UNCOMMON SENSE FOR UNREASONABLE TIMES

How to live a life that matters

By
Steve Walrath

Author of:
Cultivating Winners From Within
and
*A Divorced Parent's Guide to Seeing Your Kids:
what judges, attorneys and your ex have not told you*

Copyright © 2003 by Steve Walrath

All rights reserved. No part of this book shall be reproduced or transmitted in any form or by any means, electronic, mechanical, magnetic, photographic including photocopying, recording or by any information storage and retrieval system, without prior written permission of the publisher. No patent liability is assumed with respect to the use of the information contained herein. Although every precaution has been taken in the preparation of this book, the publisher and author assume no responsibility for errors or omissions. Neither is any liability assumed for damages resulting from the use of the information contained herein.

ISBN 0-7414-1425

Published by:
INFINITY
PUBLISHING.COM
519 West Lancaster Avenue
Haverford, PA 19041-1413
Info@buybooksontheweb.com
www.buybooksontheweb.com
Toll-free (877) BUY BOOK
Local Phone (610) 520-2500
Fax (610) 519-0261

Printed in the United States of America

Printed on Recycled Paper

Published January 2003

*"The real voyage of discovery consists
not in seeking new lands
but in seeing with new eyes."*

-- **Marcel Proust**

To my children

Donny, Trevor and Stacy

I believe in you and will love you forever

Acknowledgments

Without the contribution of the following people either via direct input into this book or through our mutual life experiences, it wouldn't be in existence.

Kathy Stevens; proof reader, editor, critic, supporter, friend, lover and life partner. It's been said "Finding someone to love is easy. Finding someone who'll put up with you is the hard part." Thanks for putting up with me now and into our future. Let's go for a cycle ride!

Carol Whitmer; You've known me since I was a youngster. As an impressionable young adult, you answered my questions sitting at your kitchen counter and then held on to me through the darkest time of my life. You said, "You're going to be okay." Thank you for your friendship, care and enduring concern. We'll dance again at Studio 54.

Pam Smith; We only met once, but the inscription you wrote to me in your book set my mind to working."Write that book!" you said. And here it is.

The core staff of WGEZ Radio: Lisa Doty, Terry Karow, Dick Boeson, Jean Whitcomb and Doug Boudry (or Chuck Riley, whichever you prefer). Our lives were intertwined with blood, sweat and tears. Without each of you, we would not have made something to be proud of for the rest of our lives. Thank you.

Friends and relation that contributed to the creation of these experiences: Alfred Kittleson, Josephine Johnson, Don and Marlene Walrath, Frank Hughes, Dave and Arnita Elleman, Dave and Lou Cook, Mike Duffy, The Krueger sisters and brother and their families, Cindy Mobley, Sandy Johnson, Bill Cunningham, Nancy Saunders, Holly Kollenbaum, Robin Smith and many more.

TABLE OF CONTENTS

Chapter 1	The Farmer's Walk	1
Chapter 2	The Scar	11
Chapter 3	On Knowing It All	17
Chapter 4	The Illusion of Control	23
Chapter 5	Risk	33
Chapter 6	Remember a Time When...	41
Chapter 7	Reality... Bites	51
Chapter 8	I'm Confused	59
Chapter 9	Beauty is in the Eye of...	65
Chapter 10	This Dream Called Life	71
Chapter 11	Look What I Found	75
Chapter 12	Regrets	81
Chapter 13	The Mind of God	89
Chapter 14	Fly Away	103
Chapter 15	Friendship	111
Chapter 16	Looking for Love	119
Chapter 17	Terrorism on the Home Front	135
Chapter 18	The Question	141
Chapter 19	Deliverance from Disappointment	145
Chapter 20	Lost	157
Epilogue		163

INTRODUCTION

Benjamin Franklin said: "Better well done than well said."

Talk is cheap and everyone seems to have a stake in the final word. But after the final word is said, why don't the resulting actions follow for some people? That's what makes living so confusing and frustrating. What used to pass for common sense and truth has been exchanged for . . . well . . . you fill in the blank from your own life.

Have you ever done your best and been told is wasn't good enough? Have you ever wished for the best in someone else's life only to be told that you're being unrealistic--even unreasonable to expect such?

Life does seem to be a lot more unreasonable and, with it, common sense can't help but be left faltering, grasping to embrace civility, kindness, graciousness and mercy. When we give up living a life with the expectation of discovering something good and enriching, we slide into what is handed to us by "experts," the sanitized, safety-enhanced controlled "experience." But with frustration comes patience. With heartache comes understanding. With anger comes resolve. With peace comes forgiveness.

Every story you read in this book is true. Every feeling and emotion is the exact same one you have felt. You and I are not oddballs. We are each unique with our own personality, bonded by our humanity.

This is Chicken Soup with a bite. The sharp spice is a memory jogged. The piercing taste might motivate a pricked conscience to change. But through it all is the abiding faith that we can be involved in a different destiny. We can work towards a healthy emotional life. We can be a positive force in a world gone awry.

This is uncommon sense for unreasonable times.

Chapter 1
THE FARMER'S WALK

"Do or do not. There is no try."
                              -- Yoda

"Do not be too timid and squeamish about your actions. All life is an experiment."
                     -- Ralph Waldo Emerson

Sweat poured from my forehead down into my eyes, stinging and blurring my vision. As I continued to shuffle along the concrete basement floor, barely sliding one foot in front of the other, I was unable to raise my arms to wipe the salty moisture away, my hands firmly held to my side with weights, 68 pounds per hand to be precise. So I kept walking, grunting and straining against the load, carrying it back and forth in this dimly lit, cell-like bunker called a work-out room. It was the basement of my friend and trainer, Frank, and I was doing something called the farmer's walk.

What a silly name for a physical exercise: the farmer's

walk. It conjures up visions of an old codger with a grizzly unshaven face, seed corn cap askew on his head, wearing tattered overalls and tall rubber boots. For him, the farmer's walk would mean carrying two pails out to the barn filled with something having to do with a farm--like milk or hog feed or cow manure. And a normal farmer would be doing this beleaguered task because he HAD to in order to eat and support his family, while I am doing this because of some deranged choice.

Frank says the farmer's walk is one of the best exercises you can do for your whole body. It affects your neck, shoulders, biceps, forearms, hands, legs . . . you name it and you'll feel it. And I'll have to say, reluctantly, he's right. Except he left out one non-physical area that zero's in on the greatest weakest of every human: our mind.

The farmer's walk is an unabashed mind game, challenging you to conquer the unexpected, formidable enemy-- mental failure. To do the exercise, you have to pick up a set of weights in each hand, 40, 60, 80 pounds or more and, with these weights dangling from your side, you are to walk back and forth across his torture chamber, deceivingly called a basement.

Period. The end.

Nothing fancy here. No neon lights, floor-to-ceiling mirrors or chrome-plated barbells. This is a no-brainer, brutish exercise performed in a dank room fashionably accented with cob webs and leaky water pipes.

I am attempting this for the first time. I pick up the arrogant weights, having defeated better men than me, and stand straight up. Um. Not so bad. I adjust the load, my shoulders stooping forward of their own accord, moving my fingers slightly back to strike an equilibrium. Like a set of scales, I'm trying to be sure the balance is just right, making sure I "feel" good and ready before I begin my repetitious march to victory. The goal is 12 completed trips across the room and back. O.K. hot shot--let's show this cowboy how it's done.

I walk to the end of the room, maybe 16 feet or so, turn and confidently stride back. No problem whatsoever. What's the big deal? THIS is what I'm paying him for? I turn and repeat the dull melodrama. And again. And again.

By the fifth cycle, my hands are beginning to tingle, little spikes of pain blitzing each finger. My shoulders are starting to ache, my wrists and forearms beginning to burn. Frank says that's normal. The weight begins to pull down from my arms, now enlisting the rest of my body, under screaming protest, to share in this experience. I turn and walk the cycle again. On the sixth turn, my breathing is erratic--haltingly shallow, catching itself, unable to extract enough oxygen to satisfy my selfish, demanding lungs. My heart is pumping blood to every tissue of muscle trying to hold this uncomfortable posture, walking and breathing, bearing my heavy encumbrance. How many of these do I have to do?

On the seventh turn, I am totally out of breath and literally half-shuffling, half-galloping my way through another cycle. My fogged and delusional thought process concludes that the faster I walk, the sooner I'll get done with this stupid exercise and move on to something useful, like passing out. My legs are aching with each faltering step, my fingers are numb trying to hold on for one more turn, my forearms are so tight they are screaming in agony for release and I still have five more unforgiving, relentless progressions to go!

On the eighth turn, I drop. I drop the weights. I drop to my knees. I drop my head down, gasping for air. The farmer's walk.

What a dumb thing to do when I don't even know the difference between a Golden Guernsey and a Holstein. My friend bends over, smiling.

"You okay?"

"Yeah," I pant out like a dog on a hot, steamy August day. "Give me a minute," and I slump back to rest against the cool, concrete wall. My wrists are cramped tight and sore. I don't know if I'll ever be able to pick anything up again or not.

As the weeks pass and every Wednesday rolls around, it's time again for the hideous farmer's walk. And here is what I've learned in order to complete not just 8, but also 12, 16 and even 20 cycles with heavier and heavier weights:

First, to begin successfully, you must be totally focused mentally. You zero in on nothing except accomplishing this goal at this very minute. Everything else in your life is put on hold--only this one task of completing the set number of cycles matters.

Second, once you have begun the walk, you select a visual, mental focal point and stay with it. As you physically begin to tire and pain creeps in on the edges, you bring yourself back again and again to whatever is motivating your walk. In essence, you are taking yourself away from the pain of the immediate moment and placing yourself in another time, another place. For me, I choose one of my children and I see them doing something. I "see" Donny or Trevor playing hockey, making a bone-crushing body check to an opposing player and, with each big hit, I'm taking another step toward the completion of my personal goal. Or I see my daughter Stacy sitting on the steps of the Field Museum in Chicago on a bright, sunny day. I'm walking towards her. Nothing will stop me from getting to her.   Certainly not these weights. With this visualization, the pain does not go away, but my experience with the pain changes. I'm able to deal with this excruciating intrusion and mold it in my mind into something positive and productive.

Third, I have learned not to accelerate the exercise. Don't rush it just to get it over with. When you begin to move quicker in hopes of being done sooner, you'll run out of air and fail every time. The farmer's walk is about pacing yourself. The first cycle is the exact same speed as the last. Not too fast or you'll run out of breath. Not too slow or you'll lose your grip on the weight. Pace. Concentration. Focus.

If only life were so easily figured out. We want things to hurry up so we'll be where we think we want to be, only to find ourselves out of breath and worn out, unable to finish what we began.

My first boss was a man at the local lumberyard named John. I was 15 years old and it was my first real paying job that didn't involve mowing lawns, hanging up storm windows or cleaning out an elderly church lady's garage in exchange for a homemade lunch. It was a suffocating day, hot and humid. I'd been dealing with cantankerous and unappreciative customers with a grim, reluctant subservience. I was ready to go home and take my sticky, smelly clothes off. Late in the afternoon I said with a sigh of exasperation, "I wish this day would get over with!" Without hesitation, John turned, looked into my eyes and said with an insistent voice, "Don't you ever say that again. You'll just wish your life away."

That's the kind of statement that sticks with you and changes you in some small way forever.

How many of us wish our life away--rushing through every difficult circumstance only to find ourselves exhausted and no better off than before?

"I wish I had more money."

"I wish I had more time."

"I wish that person would just go away and leave me alone."
"I wish, I wish, I wish . . . ."

Why do we place ourselves in the impossible position of wishing for something concerning the two things we can't ever do anything about--the past and the future? The past and the future will forever be out of our realm of control and, yet, we wish something HAD happened or we wish something WOULD happen. It's called the "if only" and "what if" syndrome. In looking back we say, "If only such and such had happened, all would be well." Or in looking ahead we say, "What if this could happen? It will only work if this and that are there!" Our lives would be in perfect order "if only" and "what if," and we wouldn't have to wish for anything ever again.

Or would we? No, of course not. We know the constant wishing would never end.

Instead of wishing your life away, choose to accept and enjoy the PRESENT, because that is something you can work with. Immerse yourself in each circumstance, good and bad, pain and pleasure, and you'll come to realize there is much to be gained from what we hold in our hand versus wishing for it to be otherwise.

The other side of this equation, the rushing and wishing for something different, is that we become paralyzed with fear, unable to move at all while holding the weights of our responsibilities. Our grip begins to slip before we've even taken our first step. We wait and wait until we "feel" good about what it is we have to do, all the while wasting our reserve of strength while standing still.

When learning how to write ad copy for the radio, I was told by my instructor: "An IMPERFECT piece of copy on the air is better than the PERFECT piece of copy in the typewriter." It did our clients no good to agonize over a few inconsequential words in search of perfection when what they needed was something in action, inviting our listeners into their store.

The key is to move. Pick up the weights and take a step. Focus on the immediacy of what needs to be done at that moment--nothing else--just what needs to be done at that moment. When the pain appears and you want to quit, you mentally bring yourself back to your purpose: you're impetuous for doing this to begin with. You pace yourself for steady forward progress. You're a living, breathing machine and nothing will stop you. This weight won't beat you! YOU are holding IT and YOU will carry it to its appointed destination.

Steady. One step at a time. No more, no less.

In 1958, Vince Lombardi, legendary head coach of the Green Bay Packers, was then just beginning his coaching career in pro football as the offensive coordinator for the New York Giants. They were playing a vital game against the Cleveland Browns with the winner taking the eastern title for the NFL. Two minutes were left in the contest, the score tied and Lombardi's offense had the ball somewhere near midfield. Snow had whited out the sideline markers. It was fourth and ten. What now? The coaches argued, disagreeing on tactics and strategy, when head coach Jim Lee overruled Lombardi and sent in the field goal team led by the powerful leg of Pat Summerall. Bad field conditions. Long distance. Absolutely unrealistic. Murmurs were heard from the press box to the sideline, "He can't kick it that far. What are we doing?"

Summerall was concentrating fiercely: can't kick it too low or the ball will sail high and short; can't let it knuckle or wobble from side to side.

Summerall hit it dead center, defying the resistance of that wintery December air, and it floated over the crossbar. Disbelief and then a thunderous roar transcended over Yankee Stadium. As he walked off the field, Summerall caught Lombardi's eye. Vince was smiling and he said, "You know, don't you, that you can't kick it that far."

Oh really? What else hasn't been accomplished in life because someone thought it couldn't be done? It's amazing what depths of uncertainty the strength of the human will can overcome when face-to-face with the doubts of the unbelieving.

Once, Frank inadvertently put the wrong weights on the dumbbells--LESS weight than what I'd been using. I ripped through all the cycles without breaking a sweat and I thought I must be Superman! Look at my progress--how I've mastered this ogre of fitness! I dropped the bars and proudly exclaimed, "I could do 50 of those today!"

Later, Frank timidly confessed to the mistake and apologized profusely, thinking the energy I had expended had gone to waste. I thought for a moment, looked him straight in the eye and said, "Load 'em up. Put the heavier weights on and let's do it again."

"Are you sure? You just did a full cycle."

"Yeah, I know. But let's see what I can really do," I said, hoping I could get through just half as many as the first time.

I focused, picked up the bars and began to walk. If my kids were here, what would they be saying? "Come on, Dad. One more step. One more cycle. We're waiting for you at the other end. You can do it." Focus. Pace. Concentrate.

Heavier weights.

Already spent and tired.

I completed another cycle.

FOCUS.

PACE.

CONCENTRATE.

Chapter 2
THE SCAR

"We are here on earth to do good to others. What the others are here for; I don't know."
-- W.H. Auden

Standing at the workbench in my dad's taxidermy shop, I leaned in with all my strength, pushing my body weight onto the butt end of a razor-sharp hunting knife. I'm 10 years old and trying hard to extract the meat out of two white tail deer feet. Once fully skinned and de-boned, I'll cure the hide, bend the joint into a 90 degree angle, sew the now dry and stiff skin around a plastic form and hang them to dry. After a couple of weeks, the now rigid feet become permanently contoured like arms pointing out from the body, hands up, bent at the elbow, ready to carry a load of firewood. Their hooves are painted black, being sure to fill each center split, and their shine is restored with a can of clear spray varnish. Mounting each foot onto an ornate wooden panel, I'll hang them on my bedroom wall as a gun rack, to the left of my bookshelves holding *Old Yeller* and *The Hardy Boys Mysteries*.

I grimaced as I pushed the knife into the end of one leg, slicing upward and forward toward the hoof. It's tough going. The skin just wouldn't give like it should, like an old piece of carpet you're trying to slice up and haul away. One leg was being stubborn, refusing to allow the knife enough penetration to cut cleanly. I dug deeper and with greater determination. With a final bellowing push, the knife lunged ahead, suddenly sliding just as quickly out of the hide and directly into my other hand holding the hoof in place. The blade sunk deftly into the soft tissue between my thumb and forefinger. The slash was painless, the metal gliding in surprisingly smooth. I really didn't feel any discomfort until I pulled the knife out and ran to the shop sink in order to wash the bright red, oozing blood from the gash. The sharp, biting teeth of pain set in, like a rabid dog clamping around my hand, blood pouring down, lost into the drain.

I began to worry. "What am I supposed to do? No one is home. What if I pass out and bleed to death? Who would know?" So I held the gushing cut closed with my free, uninjured hand and ran to another sink in the house, in the bathroom, with hopes of finding a bandage or tourniquet or duct tape . . . anything! The blood seeped, dripped between my fingers and I left a rosy red trail everywhere I went. No bandage there. I ran to the kitchen, blood drops following my every step. Nothing there either. I'm feeling a bit light-headed now, swaying like a punch-drunk boxer waiting for the final blow, when my parents walked in, their son holding his self-mutilated hand over the sink.

"Off to the emergency room, young man. You'll need stitches for that one."

Today, I have a discolored, horseshoe-shaped scar where the blade made its unwelcome introduction to my unsuspecting, left hand. It's been 32 years since that accident, but the remnant of injury reminds me in detail of that boyhood summer project of a nature-made gun rack.

The scar is a different color than the rest of my skin--it's pale, almost white. It's texture is rough and sensitive to the touch. I can still see where the pin-like needle holes were punched and the thread pulled through to bind the wound tight. I remember the queasiness, feeling frightened at not ever having had stitches before, and especially in such a scary place as a hospital emergency room. All the billowing curtains hiding ghostly secrets of life and death, beeping monitors, stainless steel carts ready with triceps, forceps and syringes, nurses scurrying from one bed to another, oblivious to whoever new might enter, bent on their own personal mission of salvation. Who was doing what? What were they doing with that big needle? What was going to happen to my unfinished gun rack, the deer legs still laying on the workbench waiting for my loathsome return?

In the end, I have a relatively minor scar. Conversely, I know of scars that are deeper, broader and more penetrating-- to the skin and to the soul. There is a scar on the belly of a man who, as a young, innocent boy, had a father who wanted to teach him a lesson. So a hot iron, evil and despicable, was placed on the boy's mid-section to sear its devilish mark. The scar is puffy and ugly . . . dreadful and grotesque. The man does not take his shirt off at the beach. The man does not talk about his sentence in Hell. The scar is a daily reminder of that horrifying time, the lessons indelibly learned, the relief that only came when the heart of his dad took one last damnable beat.

Scars remind us of who we are.

We are imperfect.

We are vulnerable

We are humans with a common link.

We all have pain.

We all have memories we'd rather efface but that are forever recalled by the slightest retracing.

Some scars we cannot see. They are neither visible nor physical. They do not leave an outward sign or mark. But they are there.

You can be sure . . . they are there.

They reside in our minds and in our damaged spirits. They are the scars of rejection. Scars of not being good enough for man or mate. Scars of ridicule. Scars of not fitting in. Scars of possessiveness. Scars of obsession and control. Scars of abandonment. Scars of wanting to break free only to be jerked back by the disheartening, unkind word and the coarse, hard heel of someone's foot upon our neck. The stinging back-handed blow across the face is not nearly so devastating as the resounding "NO" that pierces our ears, emanating from the voice we're trying in vain to please.

"Why?" is all we can ask. "Why?" is the empty, unacknowledged plea for the free expression of our own personality and individuality.

We each have scars and some are healed.

Some are still tender and in the process of healing.

We are wounded and we know its meaning.

We now have a choice. We can forever shut ourselves away so as not to be hurt again, not have our fragile existence shattered and trampled upon. Or we can become wounded healers; people who have scars and have also chosen to remember. These people know the pain because they have experienced it first-hand. They have chosen to keep the memory as a reference, as a source of renewal and encouragement for their own lives, as well as others.

One young man talked extensively to his grandmother about her fear and dread over unexpected major heart surgery. He personally knows the excruciating choice that paralyzes our minds with the physical invasion of our bodies. They share a bond that others can only look upon from the outside. Others, outside this circle of common suffering, can only give condolences and sympathy. The grandson and his grandmother share the intimacy of true empathy. They are wounded healers for each other. They remember and give what is needed for the other's survival.

I pray every day, "God, don't let me forget the pain. Don't let me forget what it feels like to lose the love of my children, to lose what I thought I loved of this world. Don't let me forget what it feels like to lose hope and purpose in life."

A strange prayer? Yes, but it is only after retracing the pain that I can then reach out and touch the scar of someone else.

And I will know.

Only the wounded healer can say, "It's true. There is life and your pain will subside."

Only the wounded healer can touch the untouchable scar and accept it for what it is . . . nothing more and nothing less.

Only the wounded healer can say, "I know the pain in your soul. I know."

Only the wounded healer can embrace and with heartfelt

passion say, "You are my brother. You are my sister. Stay with me and you will trust again."

Only the wounded healer can use the scar as a reminder.

You are alive.

Accept your scar as a common badge for others to recognize and identify.

>Then you, too, will give

>as only a wounded healer

>can give.

Chapter 3
ON KNOWING IT ALL

"The greatest discovery of my generation is that a human being can alter his life by altering his attitudes of mind."
-- William James (1842-1910)

    We stepped off the train onto busy Madison Avenue in downtown Chicago, looking up into an amazing array of tall buildings and brightly colored banners snapping from the lampposts, offset by a clear, blue sky. I was taking my daughter Stacy to the Adler Planetarium and Astronomy Museum, one of three wonderful and prestigious museums on the Museum Campus of Chicago that also include the Field Museum with "Sue" the T-Rex, and the Shedd Aquarium with its dolphin show, backdropped by myriad windows overlooking Lake Michigan, giving the illusion of these wonderful creatures leaping out of our very own waters. Stacy loves the stars and nighttime sky exhibit, and I enjoy all the historical artifacts used to scan and observe the constellations in times past. While visiting, I happened upon a most interesting piece. I read with keen interest the history of it and saw drawings of what it looked like in use. Upon leaving the museum at the end of the day, I began to try and find one for myself.

    It's called an Armillary Sphere.

It looks something like a globe, but it's not. It's circular, yet open all the way through. It has bands of metal that circle the outside and notched markings on the arch and base that support it. These markings represent the movement of the stars across space. Inside the sphere are smaller globules that encircle each other to represent a moon and sun that rotate around the interior core. In the very center, held by a spindle running from top to bottom, is one more sphere. It is the focal point of the entire artifact; everything rotates and evolves around it. Clearly, this is the most important sphere. It represents earth.

The Armillary Sphere was used in the 1600s by the brilliant university teachers, philosophers and clergy of that day to explain how the world operated. They taught, by their observation and the observations of their fellow scientists from the past 1000 years, that the earth was the center of the universe. They could clearly see this was true with their crude and rudimentary instruments. In fact, anyone could see, with even an untrained eye, that the sun rose and fell around us! The stars and galaxies and all other planetary beings revolved around us!

Anyone with half a brain knows and understands that what we see and personally experience is truly fact. Correct?

For over 300 years the Armillary Sphere was used to teach that the earth was the center of our vast universe. Respected men of that day all believed it to be true. Greek poets and philosophers going back to Aristotle and Ptolemy asserted this truth about the cosmos. Why test them? Aristotle, after all, was the greatest teacher of all time, so what sane person would question him? The Armillary Sphere was the artistic expression of that indisputable fact. Should anyone refute these tried and true observations--beware, run and hide from them! Copernicus was put to death for suggesting another explanation for the world. Galileo was excommunicated from the church and put under house arrest for the last 10 years of his life for supporting the notion that maybe it was us who did the revolving and not the sun.

There is only one problem with the Armillary Sphere. For all its beauty and artistic bends and curves of wood, bronze and iron, valiantly trying to fulfill what it was designed to explain-- IT'S WRONG! Men of reputation and respect were wrong. Did they intend to be wrong? No, they were sincere. Were their observations fabricated? No, just incomplete. Did they mislead the ignorant masses they taught to believe something that wasn't completely true? Somewhat, but not with vile intent. It's just that they believed and formed their opinions only on what they could see *at that time*. Had they been given the opportunity to use the magnificent telescopes and satellites of today–or go so far as to travel into space--they would have formed a more accurate and complete understanding of how the universe actually worked. They just didn't have the tools. They went as far as they could using the limited technological and scientific talent of the time.

The practice, however, of squashing and dismissing any opinion different than our own continued. Let's not forget the witch hunts of early Colonial life where one was proven to be a witch through careful, personal observation. By the understanding of the "experts" of that day, if a suspected witch was thrown into a lake and floated, then she must be made of wood. Wood burns and so do witches, therefore she must be a witch and immediately disposed of, usually, ironically, by burning her at the stake. Unfortunately, through this same test, one was proven not guilty of this atrocity by sinking into the water and drowning. Since rocks do not float and you did not float, you must be a rock and therefore not a witch! Congratulations on securing your innocence and salvaging your immortal reputation!

It's surprising what people will do for what they believe to be true.

Rightly AND Wrongly.

I was looking for an Armillary Sphere of my own and was given one by a friend at Christmas. I have it sitting on my library table and see it many times during the day. For all its beauty and historical significance, it means only one thing to me. It is my daily reminder that as smart as I think I am, as much as I think I know the truth by my own observation and experience, I don't know everything I THINK I know.

Steven Covey writes, "Almost every significant breakthrough is the result of a courageous break with traditional ways of thinking."

I make my observations of people, listen to what they say, see their movements and activity and base my understanding of them on the collection of these considerations. If I do not explore and consider a break in my traditional patterns of thinking, I can easily become deceived and misguided by my own wayward assumptions. Sometimes I am hurt by an errant gesture or scolded with a harsh word and leap to the conclusion that this is a nasty person, someone to be shunned and avoided. When, in fact, he might not even be cognizant of his outward display, distracted by some inner turmoil in his life. It wasn't a personal attack on me; I just happen to see a small, unpleasant hint of a greater conflict working its way through.

Conversely, I may see a warm smile, hear a kind word and feel a pat on my back, which brings me to the heartfelt conclusion that this person is my friend and someone I can trust. Actually, I did not see his hidden agenda, the real object of his outward gesture of camaraderie which was to extract a confidence or maneuver me to his point of view. I could just be a naive fish waiting for someone to set the hook and reel me in.

Let's imagine that you, and you alone, are in charge of selecting our next world leader. Here is the scoop on your three leading candidates:

Candidate A: associates with psychic healers and consults with astrologists
has had two mistresses
chain smokes and drinks 8-10 martinis a day

Candidate B: kicked out of office twice
sleeps until noon
used opium in college
drinks a quart of brandy every evening

Candidate C: is a decorated war hero
is a vegetarian
does not smoke and only consumes an occasional beer

Which of these candidates is your choice? Do you really have enough information?

Candidate A is Franklin D. Roosevelt.

Candidate B is Winston Churchill.

Candidate C is Adolph Hitler.

I will never have the complete picture with just my own observation. I cannot base my response on only what I see or hear during a specific time. I may not have the right tools to discern and understand the whole picture. I may not have a clue as to why someone may act the way he does until I explore further. I have to see things from a different view, an alternative perspective from my own. I may have to climb a ladder or ride in a spaceship to get the proper view-- to find out what is true. But how often do I take the opinions of others, even people I highly respect, rather than find out for myself? How often do I base my opinion on such limited information without going to the heart of the matter? They, too, are only working from a limited view. Could they be wrong? For all their genius and love of truth, might they be teaching me something that isn't exactly correct?

Everyone's view is skewed.

Everyone's perspective is shaded.

No one knows it all.

The Armillary Sphere demonstrates it's happened before.

"From the cowardice that is afraid of new truth, from the laziness that is content with half-truth, from the arrogance that thinks it has all truth, O God of Truth deliver us."

Chapter 4
THE ILLUSION OF CONTROL

"Happiness and contentment blossom naturally in the heart that is open. But the heart that is criticized and pressured will close and only the weeds of resentment and bitterness will grow."
-- The Couple's Tao Te Ching

"It is our hope of being a god that we desire to hold control."
-- From the Movie: Instinct

Over how much of your life do you actually have control?

50%? 75%? All of it? You can sit there and tell me you have 100% control over your life. No one can tell you anything you don't want to hear or force you to do anything you do not already want to do. Is that correct?

Let's take an example of something simple and straightforward like soccer practice. Who sets the starting and ending time which determines when you have to leave your home, put down your work or end your meeting early in order to drop the kids off and then go back to pick them up again? You?

Credit card bills. Who tells you when your payment is due and informs you your payment was late, even though you thought you had mailed it with plenty of advance to get it there on time? On the subject of mail, once you have dropped your bill payment or any correspondence in the appropriate mail slot (and who told you how much postage it would take to get it to its destination?), who controls the timeliness and accuracy of the delivery? You?

Who tells you how much to pay for long distance telephone service? Oh, you may have some different plans to pick from, 6.9 cents per call versus 6.4 cents per call, but who sets the rates from which you have to choose?

Interest rates on your home mortgage or auto loan. Your choice? Charges that will be assessed for your twice monthly overdrawn checking account that your loving partner so graciously points out with the delivery of your bank statement? Let me get this straight--**YOU** control that, right?

Let's try something else: How about when to mow your grass? Certainly you have some control over when you're going to mow! It's **your** lawn, after all . . . until it stops raining and your supple blades of grass, once lush with deep green hues that would make Augusta National Golf Course envious, now turns a brutish brown color while simultaneously the weeds and thistles choke out any remaining dignity your field of splendor ever had. Did you then decide you wished to mow?

Or you purposely made the choice to let it grow continuously all summer long, and, at the end of which you would get one gigantic, farm implement hay mower and cut every last bit of it down all at once. That is, until your neighbor complained about their children, lost and wandering aimlessly in your acres of waist-high vegetation and the city department of public works said that code mandates a grass length of no more than three inches, not to mention your mate, again, who lovingly points out that while agreeing to marry you, didn't commit to living on what looks to be an Argentinean savanna, a natural harbor for snakes, nutria and other small land-locked creatures.

So think about it. Who has control over when you mow? You? I think not.

How about when the garbage is picked up? When the full moon will appear? When it will stop raining so you can continue with your annual summer cookout now that you have a hundred people impatiently standing around your BBQ grill, holding empty plates in front of growling, empty stomachs because you're too much of a wimp to get the charcoal started during monsoon season?

How about what clothes you wear? Of course, that is a total personal choice of which you have absolute control . . . unless the temperature is 20 below zero and you wish to wear your garish yellow and pink Bahama Mama shorts and t-shirt ensemble. And your parents or school or boss or spouse says, "You're not wearing THAT!" You certainly may choose to wear it anyway and, being the fool that you are, suffer the consequences of your stupidity. So you don't even have a real choice about what clothes you're going to wear.

How about someone else's attitude? There's a good one! We each have the privilege of knowing a perpetually crabby person who complains when he gets a day off because it's too cold or it's too hot to get any work done outside. Or you give him a free bowl of ice cream and he wonders aloud why there isn't a cherry on top. You know the sort. Some of them may actually be related to you! Can you change their attitude? Can you make them happy and joyous with their life? No. There isn't anything you can do to control their outlook or demeanor. But we try . . . oh, do we try. I think in the secretive and grand scheme of how to begin new marriages, that is rule number one . . . change the other person.

> **You are hereby commanded to control and change your partner of choice. Please proceed to alter their way of thinking, modify their personal opinions, divert their ingrained tastes and demand a recount on when to switch the channel. Use any means available including, but not exclusive of, guilt, manipulation, coercion, abstinence and physical force if need be. In light of their possible non-compliance to your wishes, you may even threaten to leave and go home to mother (but a word of caution should you choose this option and find your pickup truck packed and filled with your stuff the next day, then take a hint).** -- Marriage Code of Conduct - Vol.1

We do this, though, don't we? We try to change the very people we care about. And we do so in order to control them. We do this as parents to our children, as married couples to each other, and as supervisors with our employees. As managers in business, we even get off on the idea of "empowerment."

> *"I, as your manager, do empower you to make decisions and feel in control of your life. You can't make all the decisions, just a few inconsequential ones, but you feel as if it really has an effect."*

This idea of empowerment assumes the position that I, as your manager, even **have** the power to give to you. There I go again. I'm operating under the assumption that I have that scope of control over you, my employee. I don't, and yet with just about everyone we come into contact with, the mode of operation is "change and be changed according to what is true and right in my sight and according to my perspective."

But can we? Are we actually changing anyone?

Of course not. Even those whose behavior we happen to alter for a short amount time are seething underneath and just waiting for their opportunity to tell you off, tell you where to get off or just escape--to get out of there! So are we ever really in control of any one person? No. It's just not possible.

What we are living under is the illusion of control. Down to the simplest events of our lives, all we have is the illusion that we are in control. This illusion clouds our minds with thoughts of self-determination. Self-reliance is all the rage: "It is I who dictates my life and no one will tell me otherwise."

Tell that to the cancer that just invaded your body, its angry cells working their malicious and indiscriminate damage to your once-functional organs. You can't eat what you want. You can't comb your bald scalp where once a playful crop of hair took residence. You can't walk at the same speed or go to the same public places for fear of staining your pants because you can't even control when you need to go to the bathroom. Yeah, that's right. Tell me how much control you have over cancer or diabetes or M.S. or Alzheimer's or any number of diseases that took the lives of your beloved grandmother, your trusted friend, your humble father, your next door neighbor and countless family members and friends.

Tell me again how you control the weather, determine how high the corn will grow or when a new-born bird will learn how to fly.

Tell me again, because I've missed your point about how self-reliant you are.

It's the illusion of control we exercise, not the actual reality.

We can no more control any of these natural occurrences than the time, place and circumstances of our birth. On September 24, 1883, Frank Mars was born, and shortly thereafter, contracted polio. The virus would dictate the course of his career. Because Frank was permanently crippled, he could not walk or stand without assistance from a cane, stick or the back of a chair. He wore orthopedic braces and was almost entirely dependent on his mother for each task of life, including dressing and navigating stairs. As a result, Frank didn't go outside to play stickball or street hockey. His days were "filled with aromas from the family kitchen, where he spent most of his time perched on a stool watching his mother cook."

Frank had no control over what would appear to be a terrible start to life. Yet, the very circumstances that would cause many to falter were the impetus to direct his passion toward cooking and, specifically, to the creation of sweets. Frank would go on to great success as the founder of the Mars Candy Company, eventually inventing the M&M, the number-one-selling candy in the world.

We can't make our kids become doctors rather than boost cars for a living. We can't make our spouses more loving and caring. We can't make our employees committed and devoted to their work, rather than snipping and carping at each other or "borrowing" from the cash register to the tune of thousands of dollars every year. We just can't. We only act like we can through the delusional constraints we put on them to theoretically change their hearts and behaviors . . . and what good does that do us or them? None. It doesn't last or have any real effect, otherwise we wouldn't have to keep re-inventing and re-instituting our methods of control.

The answer lies with us. Not in changing them.

We say we believe in freedom. Let everyone be free to be themselves. Yet, we ourselves choose to live within self-made prisons with fences that are 20 miles high and completely surround our pitiful little lives of control with barriers of wire, stone and steel.

We live within the fence of obsession.

We live within the fence of selfishness.

We live within the fence of anger.

We live within the fence of debt and "keeping up."

We live within the fence of victimhood.

We live within the fence of sorrow and pain.

We live within the fence of despair.

And thus, we live within the fence of control.

And we grab the barbed wire of our self-inflicted fences, even as it repeatedly scrapes and cuts our bleeding hands, and we scream with frustration. Our souls are twisted in the death-grip of our own personal hell. All because we got a peek at the illusion of our lives and saw the briefest glimpse of the fact that there is nothing we can do in spite of our determination and our best intentions. We have no control.

We have become takers.

But when will we become givers?

We have become consumers.

    But when will we be become producers?

We have tried with all our might to become controllers.

    But when will we learn to lose control?

Lose control and become tolerant.

Lose control and become loving.

Lose control and become patient.

Lose control and become accepting.

Lose control and become forgiving.

Lose control and show appreciation.

Lose control and express heartfelt emotions.

Lose control and share mercy and compassion.

Lose control and give gifts of creativity and talent.

Control and its twin brother power are, at best, only temporary. We each will die and finally, in the end, discover all the self-generated control and power are inevitably and forever lost. Why, then, do we so desperately hang onto it now?

The only real choice within our grasp is and always will be our own heart's response to what is placed before us. Rant and rave or receive and respond appropriately.

If we accept whatever hand we are dealt--no matter how unwelcome--the way we are to proceed will become clear. If we resist, our angry, fearful minds have trouble quieting down sufficiently to allow us to act in the most beneficial way for ourselves and others.

Sometimes, in the most tragic of instances, we find a minute tear in our fence. We cautiously peek our heads out into the warm, serene light of liberty and grace, and

> *"The gap between accepting things the way they are and wishing them to be otherwise is the tenth of an inch difference between heaven and hell."*

then shrink back with fear. We ask ourselves, "What will happen if I'm not in control?" Our minds race with the unthinkable, "What will happen to my carefully-constructed life if I allow just one person to be let loose?" We see our very existence in danger if we're allowed to be set free from the immeasurable burden of our expectation those whom we've taken such pain and effort to bring under our domination. And we pull our heads back, choosing the suffocating fear of loss of control instead of the true freedom that comes with accepting a life lived on its own terms, and not on our own.

Freedom is there.

It's on the other side of the fences we've built.

Give them up and step out.

> *"If a man harbors any sort of fear, it percolates through all his thinking, damages his personality, makes him landlord to a ghost."*
> -- Henry Ward Beecher

Be free of that over which you you have no control anyway.

Enjoy yourself and others.

It's nice to walk out in the open.

Join me . . . if you choose.

Chapter 5
RISK

"A ship in harbor is safe, but that's not why ships were built."
-- Anonymous

What seems risky to you? What puts a stimulating scare into your heart, sends your blood pressure into overdrive, thrusts your adrenaline to race through your veins faster than a NASCAR scramble to the finish line?

Parachuting out of an airplane? Hang gliding across a windy crevasse with nothing but air between your flip-flopping stomach and the thousand dizzying feet to earth? Swimming amongst the fierce, unforgiving sharks while gingerly feeding them scraps of their own sacrificed species, fearing you could be the next careless person who, in the future, will hail a cab with the choice of

-33-

only one hand? It could be the risk of taking a new job in a new city, knowing you'll have to make new friends while settling into a new house and having to learn new streets along with a new zip code. Maybe it's pressing the individual numbers on your touch-tone phone hoping, while at the same time disbelieving, that someone, that thought-provoking, mysterious someone who ingratiated himself into your brain last night, will answer your call, not to mention remember your name.

Risk. It has a million, a billion connotations depending on who you ask and what their experiences have been.

A young career girl, gifted with a talent for graphic design and newly married, doesn't want to leave her hometown to see if a better life can be found out East. "The pace is too fast! I'd have to drive into the city! I don't like it!" She says no to the offer, declining any potential reward of personal growth or professional advancement. The benefits, in her mind, are too small. The risk is too great.

"I just love to ride my horse," proclaims another young woman in her late 20s. "But I would never ride without my helmet," she added with a slight, almost indiscernible dip in her voice, an unconscious admission of perhaps being too cautious.

"You wouldn't ever ride without your helmet?" I ask, thinking of the fun it would be to gallop along, the wind welcoming her hair to feel the sun and enjoy the day.

"Oh, no! It just wouldn't be safe." The freedom seems too small, the risk much too great.

Football coach extraordinaire Bobby Bowden tells of the darkest day of his legendary career. He was coaching a West Virginia team when they had to play their most vehement rival, Pitt. It was the Packers vs. the Bears of college football. At half time, his team was ahead 35-8. In the locker room, he told his troops, "Just go out and don't make any mistakes and you've got the game won." They went back out onto the playing field, their commanding, seemingly insurmountable, lead safely swimming in their heads . . . and promptly lost 36 to 35. In Bobby's own words, now head football coach at highly ranked Florida State University, "People get on me for running up the score. I don't care. I'll never sit on the ball again." The risk of losing that unloseable game was so great, he avoided it and lost.

My neighborhood is like yours. I see little kids every day, not more than six or seven years old, riding around with their miniature bikes and trikes. They're wearing brightly colored helmets with shimmering, pastel stripes and shiny black chin straps pulled tight. Their elbows are neatly packaged in all-purpose pads, snug and secure to keep out wayward scrapes and scratches from inadvertent falls. Their knees are similarly bound in fortified sheaths which not only are color-coordinated with the helmet and elbow armor, but look as if they conceal all possible exposed flesh, much like a modern-day gladiator ready to defend the honor of his homeland. Forget about the disgrace of producing a farmer's tan.

These kids have so little skin showing they could be the poster models for mummy schools.

Add to the all-encompassing protective gear, Lycra pants, all-purpose, name-brand tennis shoes with Velcro straps instead of shoe laces (sorry for my nod to days past which actually meant learning how to tie laces together), and to complete the ensemble, a matching sweat suit jacket and sunglasses! Less gear was worn by the soldiers invading Normandy!

The kids struggle to lift their encased legs and swing them over the seat, the pads constraining their sincere intent to mount their wheels of flight. They finally succeed, only to roll slowly down the driveway, turn around and peddle back. Once. That's all. Then they hop off, pulling at the gear as if hornets were pummeling their face and arms and race back into the house to finish their 10th level video game. You know the drill. An hour of preparation, 20 seconds of activity and then on to something else.

But as I stood watching this spectacle of modern childhood, I couldn't help feeling just the slightest pang of sadness, a melancholy sigh. I don't doubt their parents' love and desire for safety for their beloved little ones. I applaud their concern, no doubt derived from exaggerated tales on *Geraldo* about the tragedies and horrors of bicycle accidents and how they are permanently maiming our children, disfiguring them with scars due to the lack of parental and government involvement.

SOMEBODY DO SOMETHING! PROTECT OUR TIKES!

But what that child will never know is the absolute thrill of racing that bike headlong down a scary hill, the wind snatching his breath away, whipping through unkempt hair, tears forming through squinting eyes as together, bike and child, cross that imaginary finish line. His mouth dry as a desert day, heart pounding as if a massive hand were giving gigantic chest compressions. A stitch in his side and a mighty slam of the brake, the tires skid to a looping halt, leaving the tell-tale streak of rubber, a signature of his accomplishment.

Whatever happened to enjoying the simple pleasures of life without a perpetual nagging fear of doom hanging over our heads? Where have we gone as a people when we can't cross the street, ride a bike, hop on a horse, peddle a scooter or fly a kite without checking to see if all the instructions have been read, precautions taken, terrors removed and confirming that warning tags are still firmly and appropriately attached? I'm not advocating abandoning a good-sense approach to our activities. In fact, I believe that is what we have lost: the common sense to give logical advice on how to keep from harm's way while still maintaining the ability to extract the most enjoyment out of life that we can. It's gotten to the point where we shouldn't leave the house for fear we'll be mangled, trod upon or run over in the course of our everyday living.

As my girlfriend and I rode our motorcycle through the Sunday morning countryside, she remarked, "You just don't notice as many things when you're riding in a car." She was right. Isolated from the outside world in a typical vehicle, we would never have chosen this road since it is a mundane, somewhat boring route to an even more wearisome city. In a car, she would have been asleep within three minutes and I would have been flipping through the radio stations finding something to distract me as we made our way from point A to point B.

But after her comment on the cycle, I DID look around more. The wind was warm against our faces. We could look up and see puffy, translucent clouds against a brilliant blue sky. We heard birds and farm animals as we wheeled passed, sometimes with a beep of our horn in acknowledgment. We could feel the road under us as it zipped beneath our feet, turning corners, dipping slightly left and then right, our bodies one with the excursion and the experience. We could almost taste the fresh-cut hay as we passed farm after farm on our way to a town in which we had never been--to have lunch in a funny little restaurant with a funny, elfish waitress exclaiming, "It's my turn for a table," fighting for our business and hoping for a tip. It was a morning that, by any other means of conveyance, would have been lackluster, colorless and uninteresting.

I fly in big, powerful commercial jets and in small, private airplanes. I swim in clear, shallow pools and deep dark oceans. I read exotic novels, drinking in each word picture as it forms and also scrupulously researched philosophy papers, ruminating on their context and meaning. I savor unaccustomed delicacies prepared by unknown chefs as well as relishing familiar, comforting dishes in the company of intimate friends and family.
Yet, I don't consider myself to be a dare devil or an outlandish risk taker.

There have been times when I was thankful for the watchful care of assigned and sometimes overworked angels. Like the time when ice formed on the wing of our four-seater plane while flying to a New Year's Eve celebration. We climbed and climbed, desperately pleading to nature and physics to evaporate the freezing icicles only to find ourselves plummeting back to earth, the clouds rushing past our windows as we drew our last breath, saying our last goodbyes. Skimming the startled tree tops, we landed, thunderously, with fire trucks and ambulances forming a fence line adjacent to either side of the runway, the two-way radios crackling through the town with news of an impending crash at the local airport. We landed safely, and with a profound sigh of relief.

Raising our glasses, we toasted the New Year and the grateful return of our yet-to-be-completed lives. I laid in bed that night, the darkness filling my thoughts as I realized where I had been and what had just happened with those attentive, diligent angels. It was the only night of my life I did not sleep, for those thoughts reminded me of my frailty, my weaknesses and that no matter how much forethought goes into an event, a day or a lifetime, we are still never, ultimately in control.

Risk, on some level, must continue to be an acceptable element of living or there will never be anything more discovered outside our minimalist existence. Take something as mundane as food. Subtract risk through the history of edibles, and you and I would be eating nothing more than bread and water. Caramel, for example, resulted when a curious confectioner added milk to his butterscotch recipe in an effort to improve the flavor. He discovered that the more milk he added, "the softer and creamier the butterscotch became, until suddenly, he had invented a whole new confection." Risk has allowed us today to enjoy caramel apples, caramel-flavored ice cream toppings and a plethora of delicious goodies complemented by the taste of caramel.

Risks, whether adventurous or uneventful, exhilarating or simply inquisitive, all have the possibility of broadening our horizons and making us principles in this play rather than mere spectators. I want my kids to know that it's okay to fall and bruise an arm. It's okay to scrape a knee or acquire a scar along with a tantalizing story to go with it. Living does not mean giving in for the sake of safety. George Bernard Shaw summed it up nicely by saying, "I want to be thoroughly used up when I die."

For the sake of avoiding risk, don't insulate yourself from the essences of existence.

The interaction. The participation.

The exhilarating, superabundant joy that comes from doing.

Life is not safe at any speed.

    Be smart.

        Be safe.

But be enticed.

    Because the greatest risk

        is not taking one.

Chapter 6
REMEMBER A TIME WHEN . . . .

"It is my grandfather's wish that I complete elementary school. 'You are a peacock living among hens,' he says. The phrase has an enormous effect on me."
                                                  -- Becoming Madame Mao

"Many others have traveled the same path and have left markers."
                                                  -- Richard Foster

We forget too soon.

I don't mean when it comes to holding those nasty grudges that build up like piles of rotting garbage in our brains. I know a number of people who haven't forgotten the first person who offended them or the second or the third or the hundredth . . . "Hate 'em to this day!" is what they'd scornfully say. The hurtful word, the careless gesture, the petulant attitude that may or may not have contained harmful intent, these we remember! We hang on to them like the anchor man in a tug-of-war . . . daring someone to pull that memento out of our conscious mind for fear, without that re-occurring hate, we would fall forward, face down, suffocating in a dirty pool of self-reproach and self-loathing.

Grudges. Grievances. Personal injury. Immutable injustices.

These we remember.

What we forget too soon are the people and experiences that come our way filled with positive meaning, true depth and true substance, lasting value. Our memories are short because the RAM portion (short term) fills up within minutes of our waking and then proceeds to be crammed to overflowing with each hour of our day. "Input" isn't even an accurate term for it. That's too gentle a word and implies we pick and choose, with complete self-determination, what is to be included in our memory banks. No. It's more like a giant trash compactor of the intellect that continues to smash, compress, accumulate and store millions of years of evolutionary information all in the span of a 16-hour conundrum of demanding people, confusing places and crisis appointments. And the problem is it's **every day** and it doesn't seem to let up.

The immediacy of today is the top file on the unending stack and that's the one to which we'll pay most attention. he reflections and lessons learned from the past are left to fend for themselves like the cavemen of old, holding out a solitary flaming torch with which to do battle against the ferocious saber-tooth tiger. If the memory, or the caveman, doesn't survive . . . well, it's their own fault. We have more important things to contend with.

In these troubling times, we're singing songs we haven't sung in 50 years. I honestly couldn't recall the last time I sang "God Bless America" prior to the tragedy of September 11, 2001. But it feels good. It feels like it should be here, inside me, and it shouldn't be suppressed any longer. We're remembering a time when our nationalism, our collective heritage, gave meaning to our daily lives. When as school children, standing next to our flat top desk each morning, we held our hands over our hearts, and with innocent but sure voices, we proudly recited the Pledge of Allegiance with fervor and passion rather than, as adults, complaining about the escalating taxes and inattentive city council officials, which we'll always have, ad infinitum, ad nauseam. Patriotism, by its very nature, forces us to remember. We remember with the help of symbolic terms like forefathers and pilgrims. We remember because what generations that preceded us have done now gives us the distinct advantages of the independent freedom to exercise our personal will.

We remember.

How much more, then, we should remember other events about our individual lives -- and, with that remembering, comes meaning for today.

"I have never pushed memory away. I have nurtured, not buried it. If I am the only survivor, I owe it to those who have died to remind people of the facts. I am a witness."
– Michel Thomas from
<u>Test of Courage</u>

My cousin Marj and I had dinner recently and she mentioned she has her Aunt Alice's ring, so that wherever she goes, she can carry the memory of Alice with her. I understood her sentiment because I wear my "Grandpa on the farm" ring . . . the gold one with a black onyx jewel embedded in the center. It sat on Grandpa's dresser and he would only wear it to town and to church. He was a farmer and my fondest memories that have built personal value in my life came from that farm.

At the age of eight, I was maneuvering a wagon load of hay through the double-wide doors of a patiently waiting barn. First turning the wheels to the north, then wildly cranking the wheels to the south, I was trying to get some sort of coordinated alignment that would make the wagon obey rather than rebel from my pilotage. Sitting atop the gray, Model-A Ford tractor, my feet barely touched the clutch pedal on the left or the brake pedal on the right. In fact, I had to stand straight up, all 88 pounds of me, in order to apply enough pressure to use either pedal and certainly to engage both at once. I stopped and said with an uncertain hesitation, "I don't know if I can do this, Grandpa." To which he replied with a confident voice, an air of dead certainty, "You can do it." And with that, after several more unsuccessful attempts, I did indeed, victoriously, back a wagon load of hay into a soon-to-be full and satisfied barn. As well as drive the rumbling, jarring combine tractor to harvest the oats, rounding up the cows for milking from the back woods and shoveling corn, piled high from the conveyor belt into a monstrous mound until I scooped and slid it back into the corners, filling every crevice of the storage bin. Yes. I could do it.

When being introduced to Grandpa's neighbors and friends, it would always be, "This is my helper, Stevie. Marlene's boy. Josephine's grandson."

That introduction gave my life depth and meaning. It connected me to every generation before. I felt needed and integral to the operation and success of that family unit. And when we'd come in from the fields, dusty, dirty and smiling, the grandmas and aunts would be fluttering and flying about the kitchen, preparing that evening's meal with pans and bowls making their banging, clanging sounds as if they, too, knew their purpose in life and found it in that farm kitchen. These people treated me as an equal man in the house with the same brisk instructions, "Get yourself cleaned up now. Supper is almost on." And I could eat heartily, knowing I had earned my place at the table.

My mind returns to that valued time whenever I hear a cat meow, recalling how those furry, skittish creatures were always at the back door, waiting their turn for the table scraps; the sound of a tractor sputtering to life; the smell of fresh-cut hay; or bacon frying on the stove. If I see a green bottle of Seven-Up, a bowl of pink peppermints, or even a single Holstein cow grazing lazily in a pasture, it will take me back. In spite of the heaviness life seems to place on our shoulders, it's in the remembering we can again bring a sense of our place in this world.

My grandpa would go to town once a week to visit a blind man. His name was Peter and he had been blind since birth. Peter lived alone and yet was very capable of taking care of himself, like so many past generations, blind or not. Grandpa would go and read him his mail or take him to the store to gather his few groceries, picking out a can of soup or loaf of bread to place in his basket. On certain lucky days, he would take me and the blind man out for lunch at the diner. Once, though, as we entered the restaurant, Grandpa slipped me five dollars and said I could eat at the counter if I'd rather. He thought I might be embarrassed to eat with this blind man since, because of his loss of sight, he ate rather messily... his fingers always directing the food to his fork, and afterward his face sometimes held the tell-tale story of what he had eaten: bits of corn, meatloaf and mashed potatoes. But I looked up at Grandpa and resolutely shook my head no. "I'm eating with you," I said. And I always did. Proud to be eating with a man who would care for another with such tenderness and compassion.

That's the exact reason I would immediately run out into the black, expansive field when my mom would bring me out to the farm. It didn't matter how far or how many rows of dirt and rocks I had to trip through . . . I had to go and immediately climb aboard the tractor Grandpa was driving in order to finish the job that needed doing . . . in order to be near him . . . the one who cared and accepted without reservation or reserve.

I don't recall Grandpa ever being outright angry, but you never crossed him twice. His comment would always be, "That's not how you treat people," and you would pay the severest of penalties for not doing the right thing in his eyes. He was quietly angry the morning our family moved four hours away to another city, another life. We would never again be close enough to just drop in for a root beer or come over to the house after Sunday night church service for a bowl of ice cream. He came to say goodbye and, as he drove away, I ran to the window. He never looked back, never waved farewell, his face set sternly forward, looking into a future without his "little helper" near-by.

Years later, in his final months of life, Grandpa had resigned himself to a nursing home. When I told him I was coming by, he had one request: Could I bring him a hot dog . . . with mustard.

He had a craving, an undiminished favorite taste. Maybe his memories were of a county fair long ago, with prizes for the most rings around the bottle or of laughing at an old and oft-told joke by the stage comedian. He ate the hot dog with a sublime smile and satisfied far-away look between each bite, the mustard leaving a faint, yellowish tint to the corners of his mouth. When I helped him back into bed, he turned over onto his side, facing the wall away from me, as if to say, "That's all now." I patted his hip and said, "Take care, Grandpa," and quietly left the room--the last of the family to see him alive. He passed on that night to fresh new fields, rich and ready for the harvest.

To this day, his funeral was the worst day of my life. I had been interacting with this man for 28 years, and to think he was 71 when I was born! Whenever anyone asks when the best time of my life was, I will always say, let me be eight years old again, on the farm where I knew my place in the world, where I had value and could feel a direct, elemental connection without the complications of love, money or career. It was just the fields, the tractor, the cows, Grandpa and me.

My grandma Johnson provided many of those same memories. My daughter's middle name is in her memory, Josephine. And she, too, provided value in my life at a time when I was newly divorced and my parents, church and friends decided they couldn't deal with me and cut off all communication and contact. I was on my own. But one day, unexpectedly, came a card in the mail. And in that card were these simple words: "I'm praying for you and love you no matter what, signed Grandma." The card is long gone. But the memory of those words remain, hot and heartfelt with tears, "no matter what."

Years later, when I'd go to Milwaukee and help her with her husband who had a stroke, Grandma and I would take advantage of a brief respite by going out for dinner and enjoying a brandy old-fashioned for me and bourbon old-fashioned for her. We would talk as friends and long-lost comrades in this conflict of life. We'd laugh out loud, hoot with glee and speculate on different lives, unfortunate family members and tabloid gossip. We'd then return home to care for Harvey as he spat up blood in the middle of the night or groaned from the pain of lost use of limbs and legs. When he too passed on, I stood in the door of Grandma's house preparing to go back to my job, trying to piece together my own future life. She stood quietly with her head down. I didn't quite know it then, but with her upturned eyes and tears streaming down her face, I knew that once again, for those few short months, my presence had meaning; in some small way, my life mattered, at least for now.

Grandma lived a daring and determined life for her time. She read *Cosmo*, watched Green Bay Packer games, finished her teaching degree while raising a daughter alone, and ate cheese and crackers on the couch. She was a person of substance in this modern world of superficiality. She fought cancer, won, but, eventually, succumbed to this mortal and unrelenting enemy. But her spirit of unconditional love and laughter will live on . . . as long as we remember.

"It's not about changing people; it's about helping them remember things they already know, but have put aside in the frantic pace of life."
– Stephen Lundin, Ph.D.

To be sure, these people were human. They made questionable decisions in their own lives, probably had regrets about aspects of their imperfect existence. But they are also no different than the people in your own life. They were not famous or rich or extraordinary in the eyes of the masses. They didn't soar above a basketball hoop or touch the moon. They were people who instinctively knew how to touch the heart of those who needed it most. The kind word, the hand on the shoulder, the inside joke, the wink and a smile. It was just for you.

You know them too. And they have touched you.

But you've forgotten.

You've temporarily misplaced the value they imparted to you and now you feel adrift.

All you have to do is remember. Remember that time when you knew your place and your existence had meaning. It still lies within to encourage you, refresh, renew and comfort you.

It happened and it's real. That means it can happen again . . . only this time:

"Memory and devotion. . . . you must be willing to be obstinate, and irrational, and true . . . Without this, you will live like a beast and have nothing but an aching heart. With it, your heart, though broken, will be full, and you will stay in the fight unto the very last." **– Mark Helprin**

You are the one who loves and accepts unconditionally.

You are the one who gives words of encouragement rather than judgment.

You are the one who provides a place for peace and contentment in a world of chaos.

You are the one who has a "little helper" who is looking for nothing more than your arm around his shoulder and to know he has value and worth in this world.

And others will know they are loved . . .

Because you remembered.

"Often the test of courage is not to die but to live."
-- **Alfieri Vittorio,
1749-1803**

Chapter 7
REALITY BITES

"Discouragement is simply the despair of wounded self-love."
                     -- Francois De Fenelon

I went out to eat with friends last Friday night and ended up at a local restaurant, sitting at the bar, waiting for that anxiously anticipated announcement that a table had become available for us. This is a very popular Wisconsin fish fry restaurant, so a wait of an hour or more is not at all unusual. We're waiting for the 4:30 p.m. senior-citizen, early-bird-special crowd to clear before those of us who will eat more than two pieces of perch may enter and NOT take home a doggy bag to eat the leftovers while watching *Matlock*.

The bartender took our drink order, turned and walked away. It was then that I saw something . . . something peculiar and out of place. It was hanging, dangling actually, from the back of the bartender's head. It looked as if he had gotten a haircut and the barber had missed a spot. I'm talking about missing a LONG, garish spot as it stuck out from the back of his head, protruding out to the side like a pineapple stalk. How could the barber have missed a long, spindly strand of hair like that? Did the fire alarm sound and everyone headed outside before the job was finished? Did a nuclear attack commence and the barber surmised, "What the heck--why finish now when he'll be bald soon anyway?" It was the strangest sight.

I nudged my friend.

"Hey . . . take a look at the bartender. What's that hanging from the side of his head? It looks like a Jewish peyos or something." Except that I knew he wasn't Jewish and, even if he were, there was only ONE hanging there, in the wrong position from behind and certainly not counter-balanced by a second on the opposite side of his head.

"I don't know. Looks kind of weird though," my friend replied with a twist and outstretched strain of his head to get a better look.

I know we shouldn't snicker, but it was *funny* looking! And then it dawned on me when I saw the bartender glance into the mirror with a look of dismay, and quickly take his right hand and give that misshapen strand of hair a mighty heft and hoist, and up it went . . . up and over into its rightful place. I knew then what was hanging over the back of his head.

A misplaced "sweep-over."

A sweep-over. Thin wisps of hair (there's not enough of them to qualify as a full-fledged group of hairs or cluster of hair--maybe a tuft, but certainly not a thatch of hair) that some men grow on one side of their heads until they're three miles long and then sweeeeeeeeeeeeep over the top of their fading domes in order to conceal the demise of a once-flourishing patch of hair, only to have it flop over to the other side of the head like a beached whale, thankful that the long and arduous journey was finally over and it could die in peace. It's the great

American male deception mode that no one (snicker), I mean no one (OK, here comes an outright giggle) can spot as not being the real and original placement of hair.

I saw one sweep-over on a flight to Seattle that was the most outrageous of them all. Five rows ahead of me was a sweep-over that literally began from the back of the right side of his head BELOW HIS EAR LINE and had to travel what must have seemed like 500 miles over the parched Sierra Desert in order to land on the left side of his head just ABOVE the ear line.

It DIDN'T WORK! It didn't cover anything, it didn't fool anyone. And it looked precisely like what it wasn't suppose to look like: a dead piece of week-old asparagus that should, at that moment, be blissfully floating in the great sewage receptacle in the sky.

It was awful. But he had done it to himself. And at some point during the course of his getting ready in the morning, he had looked into the mirror and said, "This looks okay. And say there, good looking. Wonder if I'll meet any stews on this trip?"

Please.

Why do we refuse to acknowledge the truth . . . .reality bites. You've lost your hair. It fell out. You're almost bald. Get over it. What did you say? You'd rather be dead than bald? As if having hair would have made you Fabio anyway. Come on!

But the sweep-over is the last step, the last breath, the last vestige of natural foliage before one succumbs to . . . the rug. The piece. The wig. The toupee.

And no one can tell THAT isn't real either. You really

believe those TV commercials and magazine ads that show a guy swimming, hang gliding and motorcycle riding with his new and improved hair and not one strand of hair has moved even one inch in the midst of these manly-type activities? AHHH yes. You've fooled the world at last. You are a man of substance, character and hair. (Money and power could be thrown in, but why overwhelm the poor little lassies? They won't know what hit them to begin with.)

STOP IT!

LET IT GO!

You look just fine. Trim it back or shave it off.

But instead, we attempt anything we can to cover it, distract our attention from it. (Don't think I was going to let you off the hook about your baldness while compensating with a beard and mustache that would blend/confuse you with any Amish farmer in the country, let alone be the lead singer for ZZ Top. Same thing, different approach.) Paint it (thank you, Ron Popeil-- yeah, no one will know you paint your hair back in with left over "Rust-o-leum" from your patio furniture project this spring . . . naahhhhhhh) and re-plant it (plugs, I believe, they're called. If the hair doesn't take, add a bit more fertilization and you have your own personal Chia head).

"The problem is not so much in poverty or wealth but in the inevitable comparisons mutually made between people."
 -- **Paul Tournier**

Ladies, don't get all self-righteous on me. I've seen women with their faces pulled so tight they couldn't go to any more auctions because every time they'd smile their arm shot up!

But we do this to ourselves so that we . . . what? . . . feel better about ourselves?

"But I have emotional needs that require that I spend this $15,000.00! I have to do this!"

Hogwash.

What you have is too much time on your hands and too much money you don't know how to spend with any amount of purpose or moral good.

Do you remember the *Beverly Hillbillies* TV show? Great fun to watch when I was growing up in the 1960s. A bunch of backwoods hillbillies move to Beverly Hills, California, because they struck it rich in oil. Sing along with me:

> *"Come 'n listen to a story 'bout a man named Jed.*
> *A poor mountaineer, barely kept his family fed.*
> *An' then one day he was shootin' for some food*
> *An' up from the ground come a bubblin' crude.*
> *Oil, that is! Black gold! Texas Tea!"*

(I could sing the theme to *Gilligan's Island* and hum a few bars of the *Dating Game*, too, if you'd like!)

They lived in a big mansion, but the running gag was that they still lived as hillbillies. Their next door neighbor, Mrs. Drysdale, the banker's wife, came by one day to talk to Granny. Mrs. Drysdale had been having trouble sleeping lately. She also wasn't eating right and didn't know which pill to take anymore to make her problems go away or which outfit to buy to make herself feel better. Granny wrestled up all 72 pounds of her bony self and proclaimed in her scratchy, raspy voice, "Spend ONE day with me and you'll sleep like a baby, eat like a horse and get yourself all straightened out."

Mrs. Drysdale took Granny up on her offer and, to her shock and bewilderment, Granny handed her a bucket and mop and started her off with scrubbing floors. Then it was on to washing windows, slopping hogs, cleaning out the oven, sweeping out the fireplace and anything else she could think of. By the end of the day, Mrs. Drysdale looked like a disheveled, soot-covered rag lady. She was worn out, tuckered out and plum spent, and finally when Granny said so, Mrs. Drysdale dragged her sorry self home.

But, the next day, Mrs. Drysdale came running over to Granny, smiling, perky and cheery-eyed, saying how grateful and amazed she was. She slept the whole night, first night ever, and she ate a wonderful full meal and she just never felt better.

Mrs. Drysdale didn't need to change her outer self to feel better. She needed to change her inner self so she could rediscover who she was, which told her what it was she needed to be doing.

My great grandma Doody was an itinerant minister, along with my grandpa Doody, traveling across Southern Wisconsin in the early 1900s. When she was in her 90s, I took the opportunity to tape record hours and hours of our family history and her recollections of a distant past. As she reminisced and recalled earlier times, I asked her about her ministry. I asked if she and Grandpa did much counseling with the folks of their flock.

"Counseling?" she queried. "What do you mean?"

"Well, talking to folks about their problems. About how they feel about things. You know, counseling them," I replied.

With a snort and a besmirching smile she said, "We didn't have time for counseling. We were too busy working!"

And isn't that the truth? Too busy working. Too busy working the fields, tending to the farms and caring for the needs of the families to bother with how they "felt" about things. Too busy with neighborhood dances and church picnics, staying up with a sick cow or trying to find the runaway horse. Too busy to ask, "What's wrong with **me**?" while looking after "How can I help **you**?"

We'd all feel better about ourselves if we'd take that perspective now and then. If we'd look around at how we can help someone else with their particular burden in life rather than spewing forth about our newfound irk and ache. Rather than wallowing around with "How do I look?" and "What can I buy to make me feel better?" how about a gift of some time at your local hospital or retirement home to make someone else's day a little brighter and happier? Maybe you need to grab a rake and a handful of garbage bags and go over to that retired person's house and clean up her leaves or put up her storm windows. Have you ever thought about taking one day a week to deliver a hot meal to someone who can't manage to cook like they once did?

Like Mrs. Drysdale, you may find all you need to feel better about yourself is to get your mind

off
       yourself.

Maybe instead of a sweep-over of our heads, we need a clean sweep of our hearts.

Start fresh. Start anew.

Then fill it with others -- rather than

you.

Chapter 8
I'M CONFUSED

"Being a Baptist won't keep you from sinning, but it sure as hell will keep you from enjoying it!"
-- Jimmy Dean

I'm confused about something. That's not necessarily unusual. In this case, however, the subject is of a broader, more elusive magnitude. It goes to the basis of why I think the way I do and how this thought process was formed by the guidance and examples from adults during my youth.

I was raised in a combination of Baptist and non-denominational churches. Both adhere to the same fundamental tenants, read from the same Bible, go to the same summer camps and basically tell you what you can and cannot do.

You **cannot** go "all the way" before marriage. You **can** kiss sparingly, with no additional physical fondling or groping, while dating.(It is amazing, however, what you can get away with in the dark, secluded back row of a crowded, noisy bus with 63 of your similarly horny friends on the way home from a youth crusade! Thank heaven for the small pleasures of life, like the enticingly salacious, emerald-colored, front-zipper jumpsuit that the more adventurous and developed of our girlfriends would wear.)

You **cannot** go to the movies. That would be sacrilegious even if attending a Disney animated feature. You, Snow White and your hot, buttered popcorn would be supporting the movie industry and Hollywood as a whole, which would only enable those cigar-smoking degenerates to make such perverted carnage as *Easy Rider* and *The Graduate*. You **can** watch some television, but **not** *Love American Style* or *The Dating Game*, as they show women with proud cleavage and wearing sexy hotpants asking questions such as, "What sound do you make while licking a popsicle?" (*Gilligan's Island* and *The Beverly Hillbillies* are acceptable. See the chapter entitled "Reality Bites" for theme song lyrics.)

You **cannot** dance. You cannot even square dance in gym class. That will require you, in full view of your snickering, belittling friends, to step into the center of the gym and hand a note to your bewildered instructor explaining how her lessons in the social graces could lead your tender seventh grade soul to hell. You would be gyrating your hips, shaking your booty and making irresistible contact with the opposite sex. You **can** sit cross-legged, in a circle, on the living room floor of your church youth leader's home on Tuesday nights, sipping cocoa and singing songs like "Pass it On" and "Kumbaya" while someone reverently, but woefully, struggles to find the chords on his guitar when, truth be told, he's two beats behind and three light years away from going on tour with Van Halen.

You **cannot** play rock-and-roll records with their devil beat and sub-woofer rhythms. That would cauterize your sense of melody and harmony (like Polka music doesn't do the same?). By listening to this modern, indecipherable clamor, your musical taste would be scarred forever, leaving you to wallow in Kiss or Foghat while trying to pay off a mortgage in your 50s. You **can** listen to the acoustic guitar, accordion or the piano, especially if it's performed at the Sunday night service by a two-man road act of which one performer is blind and the other accompanies his partner by warbling out tunes with a violin bow drawn across a common wood saw firmly pressed between his legs (I'll grant you, that's impressive! It's also an acceptable event to which you may take a date! That's two-for-one!)

You get the idea.

The whole notion being put forth is simply that there are two separate worlds: the "we" and the "they." The they being those people who do all the **cannots**. The we people do not participate, endorse or tolerate the **cannots,** as we are "saved" from all those activities, thank God.

The we people are found in church. The they people are found in bars. One sits in a pew; the other on a stool. One place has the faint smell of Pine Sol, a reminder of the efforts of the Thursday night cleaning ladies; the other reeks of stale smoke and greasy leftovers. One has a little hole in the bench in front of you in which to set your plastic communion cup after you've partaken of the symbolic grape juice; the other has a stained, Old Milwaukee coaster on which to place your empty mug and an ashtray for your extinguished cigarette butts. One has a beautiful vestibule with stained glass windows and bright, sparkling lights. The other has a dark, dank entryway with a splintered, banged-in door, a burned-out bulb and windows with smudges and smears.

Every person in one place has his face washed, hair combed and wears his once-a-week pressed dress shirt under his once-a-week navy blue suit ready to impress and share fellowship with similar-minded attendees. The other has people coming in from work/life--tired, sweaty and beat up, or going to work/life--bored and uninvolved, or who might have given up on work/life altogether as they sit unshaven and unkempt from the world's worries while smacking the dice cup upside down in hopes of winning one more round of drinks. With one, you enter the building quietly, extending a sincere handshake to fellow believers while uniting in personal intimacy with, "How are you? It's good to see you. How is your Aunt Ruth feeling these days?" With the other, you enter with a wave of your hand, a hearty "How the hell are ya!" or "Long time no see."

One has a live choir whose music you can listen to with prospects of being inspired and enthralled with their dedicated talents. The other has a live band whose music you can listen to with the anticipation of being inspired and enthralled by their customary, committed talents. With one, when you hear the combination of sound, melody and energy, you might be inclined to get up and dance and wave your hands in the air. The other, when you hear a similar mixture of texture and tones, you may also be inclined to get up and dance and wave your hands in the air.

In one, you can sit next to a friend and tell him your trials and tribulations without being judged or looked down upon. In the other, you might make a new friend and tell him your trials and tribulations without being judged or looked down upon. In one, you look to a single person in front of you to tell you what you need and what will soothe your sorrows. In the other, you look to the person in front of you to tell you what you need and what will soothe your sorrows. With both, you accept what they offer. And with both, you leave money behind.

In one, you celebrate and laugh right along with people you don't know. In the other you can celebrate and laugh right along with people you may not know. In one, you may look for solace, relief and a sense of community where you, too, can feel a part. In the other, you may look for solace, relief and a sense of community where you, too, can feel a part. In one, you receive what it is you needed/wanted and you leave feeling uplifted and encouraged about yourself and your contribution to this world. In the other, you receive what it is you needed/wanted and you leave feeling uplifted and encouraged about yourself and your contribution in this world.

In one, you could go in looking for something specific or just sit and enjoy the company. In the other, you could go in looking for something specific or just to sit and enjoy the company. In one, you remember the past, including your failures and successes, determining to rededicate yourself to a more diligent pursuit of the productive and satisfying avenues of your still-undefined future. In the other, you remember the past, including your failures and successes, and then rededicate yourself to a more diligent pursuit of the productive and satisfying avenues of your still-undefined future.

When you leave one place, you still have to face your family, your work and your responsibilities. With the other, however, when you leave, you only have to face your family, your work and your responsibilities.

I'm confused.

Which one is the bar and which one is the church?

Which one houses the sanctified and which one gives refuge to the sinners?

Which calls us to believe and which one says there is no belief except theirs?

And why are all the we people saying they are so different than the theys?

Why, again, are the we people in this world presupposing to be so much better off than the theys?

> *"True religion does not draw men out of the world, but enables them to live better in it and excites their endeavors to mend it."* **-- William Penn**

If the we people really had the answers they so fervently believe in, wouldn't they include the they's in all their activities, make them welcome as a common member of a wandering tribe, share the wealth of their knowledge and experience in hopes that they, too, could be happy and fulfilled in this temporal existence?

Wouldn't the we's be inviting the they's to come and see what they have found?

Or better yet, wouldn't the we's be going to the they's, living amongst them, sharing their disappointments and troubles, rejoicing in their triumphs and building true intimacy that only comes from a communal understanding of this thing called humanity, proving by example that what they've found is true and good?

Do you consider yourself to be a we or a they?

Should there be a difference?

> *"We can't go around measuring our goodness by what we don't do. By what we deny ourselves, by what we resist and who we exclude. I think we have to measure goodness by what we embrace, what we create and who we include."* **-- from the Film: Chocolat**

Chapter 9
BEAUTY IS IN THE EYE OF . . .

*"I wasn't there that morning when my father passed away.
I didn't get to tell him all the things I had to say.
I think I caught his spirit, later that same year;
I'm sure I heard his echo, in my baby's new born tears.
I just wish I could have told him
in the living years."*
                      -- Mike + The Mechanics

"The hand is the cutting edge of the mind."
                      -- Jacob Bronowski

    Creativity is a slippery word. It means exactly what it means to you and yet can take on the total opposite to me. I can look at something and say it's meaningless while you look at the same created work and it speaks to you from some unknown depth in an indecipherable language.

    I met an artist in New Orleans who splashed bright watercolors across his canvas, blues, oranges, greens and reds. He then took an ink pen and began to trace in lines--horizontal, vertical and diagonal--until they started to form the picture he conceptualized with just the colors alone. His subconscious, unwonted mind saw a building, a scene, some physical focal point that wasn't evident to anyone else seeing just those same colors, but he saw it. And the picture took its form. And I have "Jean LaFitte's Blacksmith Shop" hanging in my living room. A piece of art only the artist could see, in his genius clairvoyance, until it was completed for the rest of us to enjoy.

I used to scorn the creativity of others if it didn't speak to me, didn't move me in appreciation or adoration. I'd see a piece of pottery and say any 6-year-old could do that. Or some artist would be weaving his baskets and, since I am not a basket kind of guy, I would pass by with a thought of "Who would want that in their house?" And yet, the weaver would continue to weave his baskets and the potter would continue to throw his pots.

My dad has been called an artist throughout his life and yet I never saw it. He does taxidermy. You know, where you take a dead animal, clean out all of its innards and then stuff it with Styrofoam or excelsior or, in the old days, with wadded up newspapers. Stick on some fake eyes, fluff a few feathers and voila! You have the perfect recreation of a live animal--only dead.

Of course, there was much more to it than that, and I should know. I, too, was a taxidermist in my younger years. There is a required skill and artistry to making a dead fish look as if it were jumping fresh out of the water, splashing and thrashing about with sparkles of water and light. And my dad's customers always said he was the best at his work. Their prize trophies were taken home with great care to be displayed and bragged about for years to come. With his taxidermy, Dad was part sculptor and part painter with an eye for the end display, much like a window dresser who is preparing for public inspection and admiration.

Dad also did some painting, dabbling here and there, mostly backgrounds for the mounted animal displays, showing the setting sun or some country prairie with waving grass and blue sky. A dollop of paint and there would be a bird gliding across the sky; although, at the time, I found it hard to see for myself. To me, those birds looked like a mustache from a traveling medicine show man in the old westerns--a black stroke to the left, another black stroke to the right.

A bird. A mustache. Take your pick.

And then Dad tried his hand at playing the guitar. He said he wanted to be the music leader at the youth church club. So night after night, sitting alone in his workshop, with short, rough fingers made for sawing wood and not necessarily with the needed extension to reach all the chords on the neck of the guitar, he stroked and plucked, and, note by note, was able to get by. Eric Clapton he wasn't. But then his purpose wasn't to sell out Wimbley Stadium either, but to lead a group of boys in song. It was music. It just didn't sound like music to me.

And then woodcarving came along. Dad started with small birds and moved with great success into loons and eagles. I don't mean little miniature eagles. I mean full-blown, life-size eagles with great detail, each vein of each feather. It really was something to see. In fact, his carvings are on display in homes and schools all across this country. He won many ribbons and awards for his intricate craftsmanship. I don't know how he found the patience to go line by line, down each feather. It took hours and hours and hours of time and attention to intricate detail. I never was one for the North Woods look, and an animal carving was just too backwoods for my taste. I didn't quite see why people paid so much for them . . . but they did. Oh, they paid highly for his art.

As the years went by, Dad tried different forms of creation and artistry. Just now, as he enters retirement, he has taken up chain-saw carving. He takes one big old log that he's dragged out of the woods and hoisted up on its end, maybe standing six or seven feet tall, and, using nothing but a chain saw, carves out bears and eagles and owls that make others sit back in wonder. How does one take a round log, all scarred up from years of weather and nature, and extract from it two bear cubs--one sitting, one hanging over a limb--and make it look as if it were plucked right out of Wild Kingdom? You got me. And people eat it up. The upward glance of the bear cub, with his slight smirk and red, bib overalls saying right to you, "Can I come home with you?" It really is quite amazing. But I don't know how he does it and so I tended to disregard it. It wasn't the type of creativity I admired.

Recently, Dad asked if I wanted one of the chain-saw carvings and I hesitated, not knowing how a black bear cub would fit the decor of my Spanish style home--not that my home was all that color- and style-coordinated to begin with. But a bear cub?

My friend Kathy heard about the offer and said, "Well, you're going to take one, aren't you?"

I again hesitated, faltering. I didn't want to sound ungrateful or heartless.

"Ummmmm. Where would it go?"

Without pause, she stiffened and sternly replied, "That's not the question and there IS no other answer to his offer other than YES! Of course you want one. Your dad carved it and that's all that matters."

Yes. That was all that mattered.

Creativity speaks to each of us in different rhythms and moods. It may be a work of art found in a museum and gallery, or it may be something found in a garage sale or basement. What creativity does is release something inside you that tells the world something about you: what you think about; what you dream about; what you hope for. Creativity is not about pleasing anyone else. It's about giving a gift, a gift to the world, or maybe a gift made especially with someone in mind. It's the crayon drawing of a swan gliding over a still pond that hangs on your refrigerator door that only your 10-year-old daughter could make. It's the blue piece of clay, formed into a bowl, that your mother would use to place her most precious jewelry in because it was made by her 12-year-old son in shop class. It's the silver cash and coin tray made in metals class 101 as a freshman in high school that you gave to your dad to use in his own shop. The same metal tray he uses to this very day, over 30 years now, to count out coins and bills in making change for his customers. Not because anyone else would think it was a work of art, but because his son made it and that made it valuable.

And I had the audacity to wonder where I'd put something my dad made because I couldn't see the art.

It makes me ashamed of myself.

For in these very words I am writing, I am creating something. Something that maybe my kids will read someday. Maybe they'll think it's foolish or meaningless because it's not

> *"There is power in your uniqueness - an inexplicable, unmeasurable power . . . a magic."*
> **--Gordon MacKenzie**

speaking to them specifically. It's not flashy strokes of paint or glorious curves of sculpture. It's only words on paper, and they may not get it. They may not see the art. The gift.

Not just then.

But maybe someday.

Maybe someday these words will speak to them in a new way they never thought of or felt before.

It'll be personal.

And then they'll understand.

And then they'll know the meaning of the wooden carved bear cub,

hanging from a tree limb,

in

my

backyard.

Chapter 10
THIS DREAM CALLED LIFE

"Before this dream has ended, I so want to use it well."

-- from: Life is a Dream. 1600 A.D.

Dreams are a strange, perplexing element of our nighttime. They can scare us so much we wake up in a cold, clammy sweat, our chests heaving in and out from our petrified breathing. Like the time I was eight years old and I dreamed there were slithering snakes at the foot of my bed. I curled my legs up under me, tighter and tighter, in hopes the snakes wouldn't find my bare, unprotected legs. But they just kept coming until I awoke with a start, violently kicking at the sheets and blankets bundled down below, the snakes buried in my frantic state of awakeness.

Dreams can also make us forlorn and melancholy, as when we dream of people we love and miss but haven't seen in a long time. In the dream they are so close, so real, it almost breaks your heart to reach out and touch them, talk to them. You open your eyes with a distant lost feeling that someone who means so much was just a breath away.

We hear people say, "I have a dream." But this kind of dream is not from when they are sleeping. It's a dream for while they are awake. It's a dream they can make come true if they only stay the course of their desire. It's a dream of peace and contentment. A dream of a better life for their children. A dream for satisfaction in career and home. A dream of a better time, a better place. But these dreams seem even more fragile and perishable than the kind we have in the haze of night which are so quickly gone with the first sliver of dawn. Our night dreams at least tend to be remembered. Our day dreams are too quickly swallowed up by the excessive demands of life.

I feel sorry for those who say they have no dream or, worse, have lost it. It means they once hoped and strived, but now are barren and disgruntled. Was it youth or love that made their hearts and minds soar with expectations of greatness and plenty? Was it age and tragedy that brought their dreams crashing to an unforgiving ground? Can we blame any single person for taking our dream away? It's true -- there have been those who have misused our trust and plundered our innocence. Does that mean the dream was stolen as well?

Think back to what it was like to stroll hand-in-hand, seeking approval in the eyes of the one you so unerringly loved. Together you first experienced the rush of youthful lusts. You chose to put aside personal aspirations for the hope of a greater good as man and wife. You built your security in the form of houses, church and children. What was the dream suppose to be? Whatever it was, you were confident it would turn out alright.

Or so you thought.

Until the night your love walked away.

And the dream ended.

Life ended.

Or did it?

I know people who have lost their dream. They are often in the stage of life called middle age, and are broken and bitter. They put on the facade of a weak smile and outward civility. But the second their need of the moment is threatened, they turn into vicious bullies who would make one's worst nightmare seem as gentle as a nursery rhyme.

They lie, shove and snarl to get their way. Never again will their dreams be impaired by the imbeciles who stand before them. They make everyone within their circle of influence miserable because THEY are relentlessly miserable. They cannot see the light of graciousness or kindness because they blame the irreclaimable past and all who participated for their plight of resulting darkness. Their memories turn rancid as they play the role of victim. Minor hurts become epic horrors in their retelling. They feel life has unjustly robbed them, leaving nothing for which to give thanks. Yet life goes on with their unwilling consent. A forced marriage of convenience. Another child to add to their mixed bag of paternal responsibilities. Any offer of forgiveness or reconciliation is met with the stone-cold stare of delusional control and obsessive revenge.

It's all an illusion, of course. The hate fantasy. The control. The ineffectual retaliation.

But it's all they've clung to throughout these years. It's all they've kept from their sordid past of good and bad. It seems they almost thrive on the burning boil inside their soul, as if there were no other choice.

"YOU will suffer because I AM SUFFERING."

Are they justified in their hurt? Does it matter? Haven't we each been hurt in our own way? Haven't we all felt the blow and uttered the futile cry, "It's just not fair!"

So why do some survive this turmoil while others waste away? You have seen people for whom despair and frustration have become their choice of life. They sleep-walk through their days blaming, complaining and dying." Why do some go on to live happy and fulfilling lives while for others, the dream is gone forever? In their minds, at least.

Could it be that the survivors kept the dream and let go of the hate? The dream of a better time, a better place. For them, the dream is the reality of why they now live the way they do.

"We are such stuff as dreams are made of."
-- The Tempest

They are happy today because the dream is evolving. They are a part of its fulfillment. They can laugh and love and trust because they have given the dream permission to sip and taste what is possible. They can look at the past and recognize it as a part of the journey, not its ultimate end.

The hurts are lessons in a workbook.

Not a diploma for despondency.

Life **is** a dream.

It's **your** dream.

Chapter 11
LOOK WHAT I FOUND

"You can have anything you want. You must want it with an inner exuberance that erupts through the skin and joins the energy that created the world."
-- Sheila Graham

I stepped through my back patio door, onto the water-resistant, all-weather wood deck, walking past the four kelly green plastic lawn chairs and the still-not-cleaned-after-two-years gas grill and down two steps onto the concrete patio. I made my way behind the garage to my newly constructed dog house.

I confess, it's really not a dog house. It's just a tool shed on the east side of the garage: white, vinyl siding for no-painting ease, two good-sized doors that swing out to the front for spacious entry and constructed sturdily with screws and 2x4's by real carpenters. This monument to experience and craftsmanship is in direct contrast to the hack job shanty I would have built using 16 penny nails and leftover drywall that would have lasted until a feeble 5-mile-an-hour breeze came along to topple my structure, burying all its contents underneath as if to hide in shame, embarrassed at the ineptitude of their owner.

Then I would have called a carpenter!

I call it the dog house because it sort of looks like one, but I don't have a dog.

After it was built, I moved everything from the garage into it so the garage would look cleaner, less used somehow (As if I were going to take out an ad in the local newspaper and rent out the now unused space? Umm. Now that I think about the extra income . . .). Broken baskets, wire crates, water hoses, an air conditioner waiting to be repaired, garden tools, grass seed and rusty cans of insecticide, their purpose all spent in the extermination of gnats and mosquitos, all had to be stepped over as I made my way to the back, crouching over, like a miner carefully winding his way through an unfamiliar cave. Searching through pails and rags, I found what had first prompted me to leave the comfortable confines of my easy chair and take what amounts to a suburban version of a dangerous and unpredictable expedition.

A sponge. Actually what I had discovered was an old sponge rather than the newer one I thought I had. A funny-looking thing, this curmudgeon, a stinky mass of pores and fiber (I'm easily amused). It was hard and scrunched up into a dusty, encrusted, dirty piece of nothing. If I had been three years old, I would have squealed, "Ewwwww. Icky. Yucky!" and dropping it back from whence it came, run out of that horrible cave never to touch it again. But, being the adult I am, I said, "Ewwwwww. Icky. Yucky!" and promptly brought it into the house to see if I could revive it to its former state of usefulness (I am forever playing savior to something!).

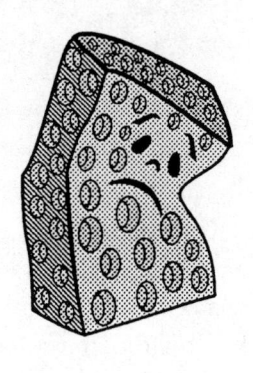

You could tell it hadn't been used in some time--months or even years. The stone-cold hardness made it impossible for water to penetrate the broken and crumbly surface, rejecting the droplets like a child rejecting a bath. Nothing getting wet here! Its pores were shallow and dry, bits of unidentifiable hair clinging to the edges. A brown stain here, an off-color tinge there. They must be remnants from a previous oil change or a quick mopping of spilled gasoline or maybe the result of natural deterioration from non-use. It's thin and dense, constrained by its own refusal to accept outside moisture. It's unpleasant to hold because I feel dirty somehow just being near it. I can't tell where it's been or what it's been up to since our last meeting, but the signs of a cleaning life rejected are all too apparent.

And that's what it was made for! Cleaning things! And here it is in its present condition refusing, by its very physical properties, to accept water or soap or anything that would again give it life. It could be useful once more. It could make my life happier and cleaner! Why, oh, why have you done this to yourself, oh little sponge? You've become this decrepit, unusable, self-defeating little piece of dust and dirt. Your existence must be miserable, because in this unrepentant state, your presence isn't making anyone else into a bundle of joy. In fact, I have no choice. I'd rather you hadn't gotten all dried out and irreclaimable, but I have to throw you away. Potential lost. A sponge not yet exhausted but, still, regrettably discarded.

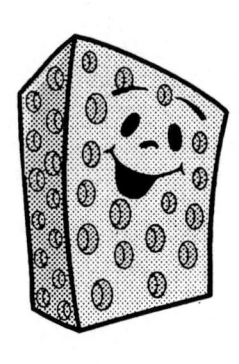

What have we here? It's my new sponge It's puffy and fluffy. It springs between my fingers, up and down like a dog on a pogo stick, jumping into space, anxiously expecting that next throw of the stick.

"Give me water," the sponge implores. "Give me soap. I'm ready to receive and be used for whatever need you may have."

I immersed my new sponge into the warm, inviting water, the soap making my fingers slippery and slick and the sponge all foamy with bursting, white bubbles. I swished it around the pail, the sponge swirling into a gleeful, perfect pirouette. Rising and falling. It came out of the water full and refurbished, overflowing with exuberance. I squeezed the sides together, twisting and bending, letting the liquid inside come gushing out over my hands, making them squeaky and spotless. Oh, you wonderful sponge! You've taken what your world has given you and you've made it better by giving it back over and over. You are a cascade of revelry as into the depths of the bucket you go only to re-emerge fuller and more potent than ever, ready to give and give again. I will use you, oh my new sponge. I will use you for what you were made. But only because you are choosing to be filled and to give and to be filled and give again into eternity. You've made my life happier, and I can now cleanse the world around me because of you.

   And I think of the people who have allowed themselves to become like a lost and forgotten sponge, all dried up. Their hard, calloused exteriors only foretell a shallow, dry existence beneath. They cannot accept the refreshing influences of new thoughts, new adventures or new conversations because they have allowed themselves to become dull and cynical, parched for anything other than their own vapid subsistence. It might even be too late for them. Just as an old sponge cannot physically accept water, maybe they too can no longer admit and absorb the elements that would renew their vitality and life. They are thin in thought, perception and spirit. They are closed up, sealed within themselves, fending off any spontaneous hint of joy or unrestrained human compassion. They are vacant and empty like the barren repugnant motel where no one is willing to stay.

   I feel sorry for them. They don't smile very much. They don't seem to like anyone, let alone themselves. We call them cranky. They make everyone around them feel just a little bit soiled and tainted. You want to wash your hands after spending just a few minutes in their presence because wherever they've been, you don't want any part of that left on you.

If only they hadn't given up. If only they had tried a new idea, opened themselves to new perspectives--challenging people and experiences that were out of their ordinary, everyday drudgery. Maybe then they would have something to give back as well.

But they don't. And it's sad, because in their own hearts they know it, too.

In contrast, isn't it exhilarating to be around people who are open and accepting? They tend to be more fun, more stimulating, tell more jokes and laugh unabashedly. They take to new thoughts and adventures like a fresh, new sponge . . . ready and willing to soak up every new idea with relish and joy. They're just waiting to see you again and tell you all about their exciting discovery. A new sport? Sure, they're game to try anything. A new restaurant, a new city, a new suit of clothes, new friends, a road less traveled . . . they are all welcome. Because the more they fill themselves with fresh new life, the more often the old, stale remnants of just existing are squeezed out, gone, banished . . . their influence flushed down the drain of rebirth, never to be seen again. They are purposefully exposing themselves to more life, more people, more families, more conversations, more interactions and more ideas. They have taken to heart "Use it or lose it."

"The creative act, the defeat of habit by originality, over-comes everything."

The most recent neurological research shows our brains are made with electrical impulses that fire between each other. These firings are the result of doing new things, getting out of our comfort zone and assimilating unique and different impressions for our brains to process and apply. The notion that we are losing brain cells because of our advancing age, and thus losing our intellectual, emotional and spiritual vitality, is just not true. Evidence now shows that a decline in mental capacity is caused primarily by the lack of mental exercise. John J. Ratey, M.D., points out that "Every time we choose to solve a problem creatively, or think about something in a new way, we reshape the physical connections in our brains. The brain has to be challenged in order to stay fit, just as the muscles, heart, and lungs must be deliberately exercised to become more resilient."

Dr. Ratey goes on to suggest that we have the best chance of growing the connections between these firings by tackling activities that are unfamiliar to us, such as learning a musical instrument, repairing engines, studying philosophy or delving into conversations with provocative people. By avoiding uncomfortable situations, we lose the ability to try and accept and renew through learning and participating with life. If we constantly challenge our lives, it is now scientifically shown that we can "delay the onset of Alzheimer's disease, recover from a stroke, and live a longer, more interesting life."

The old sponge didn't lose its flexibility because of its lack of capacity, but because it didn't use and nurture what it already had.

When we don't use what we have, we lose our reason for being.

We dry up.

Chapter 12
REGRETS

"The quality of mercy is not strain'd . . . It is twice blest: It blesseth him that gives and him that takes."
-- Merchant of Venice

There comes a time in everyone's life when we must forgive our parents.

Sounds a bit odd, doesn't it? After all, it was our parents who gave birth to our existence. They clothed, fed and provided for our every need when we were unable to do so for ourselves. They guided, nurtured, disciplined and shaped our behavior and point of view to ones they felt would serve us best. Sure, they made mistakes. With time, maybe even second-guessed some of their own parental decisions. But forgive them?

For what?

When I was a teenager, I had a favorite and often repeated saying: "I have absolutely no regrets about anything I have done. I made the best decision with the best information available at the time. I have absolutely no regrets." A pretty easy thing to say when the worst thing you've done up until that point in your life was stay out past midnight or cuff your sister upside the head when you were put in charge of babysitting.

But what about later in life as you get into your 20s and 30s? I'd gotten divorced, started a new career in a different city. Decisions were made and hard choices struggled through. Yet, I said the same thing, "I have no regrets. I did the best I knew how at that time." I still felt it was a valid statement. I had made my bed, so to speak, and was sleeping quite soundly. Here I was. So be it.

Except that now, my naivety has passed and my self-proclaimed innocence has a hollow feel to it. I can't see my kids as much as I'd like. A comfortable, casual, adult relationship with my parents never really developed to its fullest extent. I look back, not with a forlorn desire to do everything over, but with a greater sense that I could have made a better choice. I could have chosen a course that would have been more beneficial to everyone involved, including myself. If only I had made the effort to think for myself rather than rely solely on my past, well-intentioned verbal and model instruction.

I find it difficult and unsettling to realize that, as adults, we make so many of our choices based on our parents. Their values, influences and norms all have conspired to make us one of them.

As my dad was a product of the culturally conservative 1950s and his parents were a generation from the Depression, he didn't learn how to relax and be himself, to be comfortable with his personal role in life, community and even family. His ingrained substance was a reflection of his own unbroken connection to a past era, defined by hard, physical labor, few encouraging words and little emotional support. Positive feedback was rationed like butter and sugar was in the 1930s.

Scarce in supply. Portioned out with reluctance. And only for rare and exceptional reasons.

"Don't spread it around needlessly that he's actually doing well at something. It'll only give him a big head. I don't know why he thinks so highly of himself. There are so many areas that he isn't measuring up."

As a result, I took the cue that you withhold yourself, burrowing down like a phantom mole, poking your head out, only out of physical necessity lest you get vilified by the errant, mis-spoken thought or misguided hormone. Hide your true aspirations. Stay in your room. Keep to yourself and think about the consequences before you ever open your mouth when at home. Watch TV, read a book, in fact, read thousands of books, and your opinions, theories, sentiments and subjective beliefs will be developed incognito. Don't let the real you, the inside you, come to the surface or it most certainly will not live up to a now long-running list of expectations linked by a common bloodline.

"Can't you see how you're hurting your mother? Why are you doing this? I can't talk to you. Here's a letter I left on your bed. It will lay out for you exactly why I don't think you're a very good person. Good people don't do the things you do, like wanting to go to a softball game rather than Sunday night church.

Hey, thanks for the Father's Day note, telling me you love me and all. But why can't you love your sister more? But let's not talk about it. Just do what I say, or better yet, do what I'm teaching this week in Sunday school class. I do set a good example for you, don't I?

Oh, and I found this book on the stair. You're reading this trash? It's called *Looking for Mr. Goodbar*. I don't want this in my house. Get rid of it . . . NOW! But we don't have to sit down and talk about it, do we?

And by the way . . . it would be nice if once in a while you just said thank you for all the times we have to pick you up from basketball practice. Just once. Have I ever seen you play? Well, no. I'm preparing my lesson plan to teach the inmates in jail about God.

And one more thing . . . your mother and I don't think you treat your girlfriend very well. She needs more attention but you're so busy with everything. She is such a nice girl. Why can't you be nicer to her?

Yes, all I do is turn my back and fiddle around at my workbench while you stand there in your white T-shirt, head down, eyes bleary from a sleepless night, trying to tell me why you're getting a divorce. No, I would never get a divorce. What did I do to make you think this is any way to live? While we're at it, I'm glad your grandmother didn't live to see you divorced. It would break her heart.

Do I have any regrets in life? No, I don't. Well, just one. I wish I had bought my sister a harp that she wanted. She said she'd like a harp, but then she died and I always wished I had bought her that harp. No, no other regrets. I'm pretty happy with how my life turned out."

And as I thought about my father's statement, "I'm pretty happy with how my life turned out," I reached deep in my brain, searching for some relevant meaning to his declaration that he had no regrets. Is this a life to be envied or pitied? Is the ideal scenario to come to the twilight of your time, mortgage paid in full, your natural teeth intact, saying to yourself, "I did alright?"

. You have no regrets about not talking to me? No regrets about wishing we had spent more time together? No regrets about getting to know this person who spent 18 years under your roof, eating your food, sweeping out your garage? No regrets about discovering who this adult man is that bears your name? Your only regret in your WHOLE LIFE is that you didn't buy a harp for your sister? Do you ever think that just once I would liked to have heard, "I'm proud of you. I enjoy your company. I think you turned out to be a terrific person?" But if YOU have no regrets, then I guess I don't either.

But I do.

I do now.

I have regrets for not being kinder or taking the extra time when someone else needed it, time that would have made me late but could have changed a life forever.

For lack of one minute.

I have lots of regrets because, as I look at how things stand, I truly want to do more, be more, help more, experience this life more. St. Augustine said, "Therefore, be always unhappy about where you are if you want to reach where you are not. If you are pleased with what you are, you have stopped already."

Regrets of the past don't weigh me down. They spur me forward with a roaring cheer from the sideline crowd to make better choices, use time rather than lose it and, with a clear, irrefutable view, make a difference. As exemplified in *Saving Private Ryan*, wherever my mission might take me, despite uncertainty of the specific path, my objective is steadfast, unmovable--to win the war. Regrets drive me to talk to my kids like normal people talk, not like a generational mandate of code and conduct. They make me ache to be with people I love, to sit down, relax and ask what's going on in their busy and harried lives. Regrets make me want to know what you're thinking, how you're feeling, what's going on that is causing you to be ecstatically happy or pressing your soul down with an unbearable weight of desolation and despair.

I know a family who called the authorities to have their only son arrested and taken away. He was 19, going on nowhere. Without ambition or a high school diploma, all he had were his disreputable buddies, his color television set and a stolen cell phone so he could look cool. Unknown to anyone else, he also had a batch of outstanding criminal warrants, truancy violations and a partially wrapped joint found under his car seat from a previous police stop. Unknown, that is, until his parents, aching to see him get straightened out, gave him a choice: get a job or get out. Learn what life is really like when you're hungry and on your own. He made the choice. The police were called. With his arms immobilized, handcuffed behind his back, he was led out of the house, tears streaming down his face, his mom and dad, good people, in anguish.

He's been sitting in jail now for a couple days. Probably shocked and confused at the seeming betrayal by his parents. Will he learn his lesson and find destiny in a 6 x 8 concrete cell? Will he come to hate his parents, seeing them as uncaring, phlegmatic, undeserving of his kinship? Or will this young man see the reality of what this situation really is: a child on the edge of a dark, lamentable life, so close to losing it all, and two loving adults, doing what they think is best with the information, advice and historical perspective they have, trying to make it alright.

Do you think they will talk about it when he gets out?

Will he forgive his parents?

Should he have to?

I've forgiven mine. My parents were doing what came naturally through their own bloodline and upbringing, but not necessarily from their own heart and conviction. I realize that. They did the best they could with what they felt they knew.

> *"Regret for the things we did can be tempered by time; it is regret for the things we did not do that is inconsolable."*
> **-- Sydney J. Harris**

There will come a day when I will need the forgiveness of my own children. The best of intentions have fallen short. I have disappointed them. I have unintentionally made them doubt their world, and quite possibly, themselves. I have caused wounds.

But I love them.

And I want them to know that, as unbelievable as it may sound to them, they will need the forgiveness of their children.

Maybe if we can all get our heads around this thought, that we all have and will fall short, that we all need and crave forgiveness at different points in our lives,

then in these moments now we have together, we'll be able to relax a bit,

allow our honest selves to be shared,

accept and enjoy each other more . . .

. . . and talk.

Chapter 13
THE MIND OF GOD

"One person with belief is equal to a force of ninety-nine who have only interests."
-- John Stuart Mill

God's Word, as accepted by faith, no matter what your religion, has been recorded by human hands and minds for centuries. Carved in stone, etched across scrolls or inked on paper, God's Word (or Words) have been passed down to us living in the here-and-now via many forms and fashions. I am not attempting to assuage your specific view of God's Word or the vehicle by which you study and worship God.

What I am offering here are simply questions. Questions that make me wonder if God has these thoughts. Questions I might be asked if I were God.

I may be way off base here, and I don't mean to imply I have any special mandate to write my own interpretation of the Word of God. I am not, however, so afraid of these questions that I think God would be offended by these musings. In all His power and glory, I'm confident God is not troubled by my elucidations of what He has already attempted to say or that my queries will bring a subsequent inadvertent change in the course of human lives. I think He's bigger than that.

I'm not trying to answer your personal questions about God either. I believe we each, with personal integrity, must work out our faith about God, as guided by His Holy Spirit and Son, Jesus Christ, and that if we truly seek, we really will find. I'm just tired of going through a third party all of my life when trying to understand the mind of God.

The church has its place in helping me **to** God, but in too many instances, I find in history and personal experience, the church loves to think of itself as the voice of God. The ONLY voice of God, even to the point that it is the exclusive way to God with all its opinions, doctrines, practices, rites and customs. This is the traditional view. Parents, written commentaries, elders, television evangelists, priests, friends, prophets, fortune tellers . . . all claim they are telling us the word of Almighty God.

That MAY be true.

I don't dispute their intent or faith.

I merely propose a more radical view.

Go to God directly.

Then I will be going to the source, the center, the foundation of something basic and true.

> *"The desperate need today is not for a greater number of intelligent people, or gifted people, but for deep people."*
> **-- Richard Foster**

Some may say I am mocking God with these thoughts. "Would plague and boils tear at the vitals of anyone that asked out loud . . . " I can only assure you one does not make fun of that which one truly desires to know. And so with trepidation and careful consideration, I offer the following:

*Do you think
God
ever wants to interject with
"Could I say something?"*

Do you think
God,
in retrospect,
might consider
"Next time,
I'd do things differently?"

Does
God
ever brag saying
"For people -
they're kind of cute?"

I wonder if
God
is
amused or disappointed?

Does God ever turn to Gabriel and say "What was I thinking?"

I wonder
if
God
Laughs?

Do you think
God
ever wants to just say
"Stop it!"

**Do you think
God
ever wants us to pause from our
talking
singing
testifying
preaching
proselytizing
confessing
crying
complaining
and sit still
for just
one
minute?**

Does
God
have a preference
in music?

*Did
God
invent the
concept of lawyers
or
did man?*

Does
God
ever shake His head
in exasperation?

*When we cry out
for help, -- will
God
ever say,
"Who are you?"?*

When I die --
will I be surprised by
who is in Heaven
and
who is in Hell?

Does
God
ever want to shout
"How much plainer do you
want me to say it?"

What does God hate most?

If God's Word is truly universal, why is there ANY divergent interpretation?

If God misses us so much -
why did He do this
human planet Earth thing
and not
just keep us
all together in Heaven
to begin with?

DOES GOD ACTUALLY ROOT FOR ONE SPECIFIC TEAM?

Is God saddened by the influence of money?

God's Top Ten Reasons why He should flood the Earth and start over for a 3rd time:

10) Ego (His)
 9) Divorce
 8) Obstinance
 7) P.E.T.A.
 6) Tofu
 5) War
 4) Child Abuse
 3) Home Shopping Network
 2) Ego (ours)
 1) "NOW they'll believe"

Do you ever wish you were God?

Chapter 14
FLY AWAY

"There are three kinds of men. The one that learns by reading. The few who learn by observation. The rest of them have to pee on the electric fence for themselves."

-- A Cowboy Creed

I was on a commercial flight last week, sitting quietly, browsing through my books and study materials for the next day's seminar, as the plane gently lifted off the ground and nosed into the heavens to fly among the other celestial beings. 10,000, 20,000 and finally our cruising altitude of 33,000 feet was attained as announced by the authoritative, disembodied voice of the captain. Our route was described in the trademark lingo of pilots everywhere, noting landmarks and cities we would be passing over, confirming in my own mind that this was where I really wanted to go, and I settled in for the three-hour journey (in contrast to the preparation for a three-hour cruise, in which case I would have packed more books, a grass skirt and lifetime supply of batteries for the radio that would announce my rescue from an uncharted desert isle. I looked around the plane. Alas, Mary Ann and Ginger were not to be found, although plenty of Skippers and Mr. Howells were on board.).

When suddenly something whipped past my head!

Buzzing and dodging back and forth . . . up and then down . . . there it was again!

What could be flying around inside an airline cabin at this altitude?

One more time, right past my head again, buzzing right up the center of the aisle. A fly--a common household, irritating, son-of-a-gun, picnic-invading fly was buzzing up and down the aisle of a 767 jetliner bound for the West Coast! It was the funniest, strangest, surreal sight to be flying at 33,000 feet and now start thinking about bringing a fly swatter as a carry-on! Think of the story you'd need to have prepared when THAT is examined by the security x-ray people.

"Uhhhh. Yeah. You see, your airline has a real pest problem, and I never travel without my personal fly swatter anymore," as they turn their heads in a sideways glance to hide the snicker and snort produced by your fantastic story.

"Wait'll I tell the guys at the bar about this one!"

But here it was, just an ordinary fly, swishing and buzzing up and down the aisle as if it didn't have a care in the world. As if it were waiting for the beverage service to begin so it could sit on a newly opened can of ginger ale, sip and enjoy the ride.

"Did you want ice with that drink, Mr. Fly?"

Did the fly?

Imagine the shock when that fly was just minding its own business, buzzing around cold, snowy Wisconsin looking for any place warm to snuggle in for the remaining winter when it happened aboard this long, metal tube filled with a 100 people or so. ("Hey! Do you people have room for me to warm my toes for a bit? This looks more like a theater seating arrangement. I wonder what movie is playing? Oh, well. Let's check it out anyway.")

I'm sure the fly banged its head on the windows a few times, as flies do, in order to get out (would he have been in for the ride of his life if he had succeeded at 33,000 feet!). And then, finally, settled down for a short nap. Suddenly, the doors miraculously opened and, "WOW--it's now 85 degrees, and look at the sunshine! Someone hand me my shades! HOLY COW! Where did I land? What the heck just happened in this time tunnel? This never happened when I flew out of the house before!"

Imagine the confusion, the excitement, the fear and exhilaration at entering one world and coming out into something totally and absolutely different. This wasn't at all what that fly expected! This wasn't at ALL what he anticipated! It was the best Twilight Zone episode ever imagined!

It was never his intention to see a new and foreign land. He was just flying around, checking out the scenery in his normal universe of a half-mile circumference from where he was born. He was just looking for a nice mate to cohabitate with or for a bite to eat. But here he was. The land of milk and honey (or is heaven garbage and waste for a fly?).

NOW what should he do?

Leave the plane and do some sightseeing?

Stay put and hope this big bird goes back where it came from?

Holler for help?

What should he do?

Have you ever thought you were going one way only to find yourself arriving at a completely different destination? You had everything planned out so well. Go to college, meet your sweetheart, get your degree, get a great job, have 1.5 kids and settle in for a predictable and ordinary life.

And then something happened.

What was it?

Did you meet someone unexpected?
    Was your bus late?
        Did you run out of money?
            Were you offered a ride?
Did you take that job or turn it down to move out of town?
    Were you hurt in an accident?
        Did you fight for your life?
           Did you change your mind?
Did you look in a certain direction?
    Did you say the wrong thing?
        Did you turn a corner?
           Did you accept the invitation?

Did you go with your gut?
　　Did you stop out of fear?
　　　　Did you explore out of curiosity?
　　　　　　Did you desire to slow down?
Did you take advantage of the situation?
　　Did you go where you'd never gone before?
　　　　Did you refuse to participate?
　　　　　　Did you lose your heart?
Did you regain your senses?
　　Did you follow a fantasy?
　　　　Were you ready to accept reality?
　　　　　　Did you say "yes?" Did you say "no?"
Did you say "let's wait?"
　　Did you say "let's go?"
　　　　Did you do something stupid?
　　　　　　Did you do something fun?
Did you do the right thing?
　　Did you let the change go by?
　　　　Did you tread on thin ice?
　　　　　　Did you seek safety on the shore?
Did you appreciate true talent?
　　Did you accept the easy offer?
　　　　Did you ask a question?
　　　　　　Did you find what you're looking for?

One never knows where life will lead and, most certainly, it will lead to places never dreamed of.

We impose this same expectation on other people, as well. We have an idea of where they should be going and what they should be doing, but the reality is that we haven't a clue! I was once asked, "Do you know how to make God laugh? Tell Him your plans for tomorrow!"

Think of this poor set of parents. Their son was a loser.

- He didn't start talking until he was three.
- He didn't like school so he quit at age 15.
- He didn't pass his high school G.E.D.
- When he did finally pass, he went to college and cut most of his classes.
- When he did finally graduate, it was because a friend lent him his class notes.
- Then he couldn't get a full-time job.
- He finally took a job as a clerk in a patent office and stayed for seven years!
- And four years after a major breakthrough in his career, he returned to his old school to say hello to the headmaster. Remembering how poor a student he was, the headmaster thought his former student had returned to campus to beg for money or food.
- Instead, the student wanted to share his theory . . . $E=mc^2$.
- And that same year, 1905, he developed the quantum theory of light, published two articles that together proved the existence of the atom and, later in the year, made an addition to his theory of special relativity.

Poor Mr. and Mrs. Einstein. Their little fly was not going anywhere they could see when, in fact, Albert was on the trip of a lifetime. Just not on the same plane as his parents. Or the rest of the world, for that matter!

Take a look at Galileo's law of inertia:

A body continues to do whatever it is doing until something comes along to force it to do otherwise.

How many of us just keep going along the same old path, doing the same old mundane tasks day after day, year after year, only because it's the easiest thing to do? It's human nature. It's more convenient that way. It takes something to come along to FORCE us to do otherwise.

Good or bad.

Richard E. Taylor was the 1990 winner of the Nobel Prize in physics. As he recalls his life:

"I assumed that I would probably be a surgeon, but my grades were not nearly good enough to go into medicine. Actually, I blew my fingers off in an accident. Later, this doctor that lived next door said to me, 'Look fella. People aren't going to have much confidence in a surgeon with half his hand gone.' And I said, 'Gee, I never thought of that'!"

You see, it's important you don't hold onto the wheel of your car too tight. You never know where the road might take a turn on you.

Go with the road and let it take you to places you never planned.

Loosen your grip.

Flex your instincts.

Follow your opportunities with glee and enchantment at discovering the unknown.

The unknown world

Your unknown heart.

Fly away . . . .

    Fly away . . . .

        And take the trip of a lifetime.

Chapter 15
FRIENDSHIP

"It's a poor friendship that needs to be constantly bought."
-- German Proverb

He was wearing a blinding, bright yellow suitcoat and pants, the brilliance of it so loud that you want to put your sunglasses on but you'd still have to squint, even in church. Add to this ghastly ensemble a white belt, white saddleback shoes with gold buckles and, what else, white socks. The tie is a nondescript pattern of faded yellows and browns, looking as if it had been dipped in an open can of vegetable soup and hung on the clothesline to dry. His hair was always thin and his forehead always a glistening globe susceptible to too much sun and too little protection. He smiled easily enough. Laughed fairly often. His wife was a happy, bouncy sort, usually dressed in pearls and brightly colored patterns of sunflowers and daisies or some other garden-like tones and shapes. She was a joker, a teaser and a flirt, at least a flirt as far as a conservative Baptist minister's wife **can** flirt, which means nothing more than a wink or a poke in the ribs.

From ages 10 to 18, I spent more time with them than any other people in my life, including my parents and friends. They were my pastor and his wife. They were my confidants in the confusing, whirling teenage years. I talked to them about life, religion, philosophy, girlfriends and the state of current music. ("Brandy" by Looking Glass and "Joy to the World" by Three Dog Night were radical songs then, and both were perceived to have the power to topple our government and test the moral fortitude of our families. The question in my family was, "What's wrong with the 'Joy to the World' we sing at Christmas?") It was their 1966 beige Cadillac I drove to Florida when he was graduating with his doctoral degree. I, all of 16 years old with a newly minted driver's license, tagged along as the invited guest to this special event/vacation.

We cried together. Ate together. Read together and talked together. For adults, they were pretty "with it" people. For a Baptist minister and wife, you might even say they were contemporary, considering they didn't have any children of their own. I obliged as their stand-in kid with fastidious church attendance, reliable leadership for the youth group, enthusiastic direction of songs during the Sunday night service, creative game czar for Vacation Bible School and actually filled in with a sermon or two when the pastor was gone for a weekend.

He was the first person I met when we moved to Rhinelander, Wisconsin. Within hours of cruising into town, I had fallen out of a tree, broken my arm and he, as a local pastor, came to say hi, read a bit of Scripture and pray for my fast healing. He baptized me, prayed with me, taught me and married me. He was my friend, even after I had left his church to pursue career opportunities in other cities. He and his wife wrote, phoned and we enjoyed the occasional meal together when time permitted during visits home.

At the age of 28, I made the excruciating decision to move away from my wife and family to take over management of a radio station some 100 miles away. The resulting dissolution of our relationship and the aftermath of our inevitable divorce was cataclysmic to my parents, my church and this pastor/friend of mine. Each and every week, he and his wife would faithfully make the drive to where I was living to talk, to reason with me, cajole me and encourage me to return to the church, return to my family, and find a way through this dark time. Prayers, pleadings and firm resolve could not, would not move me from my position at that time. After several months of these weekly visits, they suddenly and inexplicably stopped.

They stopped calling. They stopped visiting. They stopped writing. They just stopped. I didn't pursue them and they didn't pursue me. For my part, I needed a break, some time off from this manufactured existence, not of my construction and design, but of those who would call themselves my protectors and guardians.

But I would think of them from time to time. I heard that he had left his Baptist church in Rhinelander and taken another congregation somewhere. As I understand, that didn't last too long. Then I heard he had left the pastorate all together, no church desiring his leading, no flock clamoring for his teaching. Last I knew, he was working at a glove factory in a sleepy little town out in the rural countryside.

One afternoon, after several years and several job changes of my own, I was sitting in my tattered red rocker, looking out the window of my small, two-bedroom apartment when a whim, a flicker of an idea peaked my curiosity. Its persistence pricked my conscience and I thought it wouldn't take very much effort to see if I could find this pastor/friend of mine. "I wonder what he's up to? I wonder how they're doing? I wonder if they still remember this prodigal son who has now grown and matured to have a soul of his own making?"

I called information to get their number. Yes. They're still living in that same small town and their number was read aloud down the telephone line by that eerie, automated pseudo-female voice. 715- 478- _____. With a slightly trembling hand, I pressed each keypad, hoping time travel would not find me disappointing to a formerly, enthusiastic advocate.

One ring. Two rings. He answered. After the "Hey, what's up? What's going on? How's life?" sort of banal conversation, we soon ran out of things to say. I hurriedly gave them my telephone number and address where they could find me and said, "Give me a call. Let's get together." And I meant it. Maybe seeing them in person again would re-stir the elements of communion, camaraderie and unforsaken belief. I reached out to revive a once strong connection.

I never heard from them.

Ever again.

Today, I don't know if they are alive or passed on to that rapturous place that meant so much to them. You've heard the phrase about some people that they are "so heavenly minded they are of no earthly good." Was he sincere in his worship of God? I'd have to say yes. Did that mean he could no longer be a friend of mine because I could not do what he wanted me to do at a time in my life when I needed extreme examination and excavation of my beliefs and convictions? He wanted me to do what any sane person desired for me: to straighten up and fly right. Come back to the flock. Come back to your home. Come back to your loved ones. Do what's right. Do what is good for you. Do what you're suppose to do. Do what the church says. Do what God says. Do what your parents taught you to do. Do what our friendship dictates that you must do . . . or . . . we . . . can . . . not . . . be . . . friends.

Is that what friendship is? Doing only what your friend wants and expects you to do? What happens if you, the other party in this relationship, lose your way? What happens when you have to question and challenge those things that have become mundane and irrelevant, no matter how theoretically truthful? Even something so ingrained as our soul's destination, our life's purpose and our function in this mortal, temporary place? What happens when your struggles are not understood? Who can you turn to when family and foundation are rocked and rejected, if not our friends? I thought friends accepted you no matter what your agreements or disagreements. I thought friends relied on the value of your created humanity and not on the rituals of social or theological repetition.

Was he telling me that because I could not do, I chose not to do, what he wanted me to, then I had no value? I had lost my eternal reason for being because of his denial of my outward actions? Is that what God, YOUR God, YOUR ministry, YOUR church policies dictate?

That I now have NO VALUE?

I didn't say you couldn't disagree with me. I didn't say you couldn't point me toward a smoother path. I didn't say you had to parade me in front of the masses as a shining example of fidelity and unreserved truthfulness, but does that mean you won't call me? You won't talk to me? You won't reconnect on any level? You mindfully, deliberately, morally, ethically, intellectually, spiritually CHOOSE not to be my friend?

Then please tell me . . . of what **earthly** good are you?

If God can say, "I love you. Come to me just as you are," then how can you say you won't even be my friend, let alone a friend in need? In all your superior humanity, as a self-proclaimed leader of the church and self-proclaimed voice and interpreter of God's Word, what you're really saying is, "I will bypass God's love and forgiveness for you and instead choose MY judgment of you. I judge you and thus proclaim you to be of no value, to me anyway."

This couple had given me a small picture book, filled with photos and captions from that Florida trip where he received his doctorate in Religious Studies. In the front of the book they wrote, "'To our Timothy,' from Pastor Dave and Arnita." Timothy was the protegee and student of the Apostle Paul. Paul and Timothy were friends. Paul even begins a letter by saying, "To Timothy, my true son in the faith . . . ." Later in the letter, the Apostle Paul urges Timothy to command certain men not to teach because, "They want to be teachers of the law, but they do not know what they are talking about or what they so confidently affirm."

Maybe the glove factory was God's way of telling this pastor to stop the meaningless talk.

In the back of the picture book is another inscription. "Thanks for the memories" and again their names.

Yeah. Thanks for the memories. Of friends who couldn't see beyond their worship. The pew was bigger than their passion. The attendance record of a church service of greater value than the absence of a wanderer.

As a priest, Karl Malden was confronted with his true calling in the classic movie *On The Waterfront*. In his first encounter with the brutality of injustice through the murder of a parishioner, he attempted to comfort the sister by saying,

"Time and faith. Remember, time and faith. I'm in the church if you need me."

The sister, played by Eva Marie Saint, was lying over the body of her dead brother, only minutes before being thrown off the roof of a towering building for defying the mob-run labor union She looked up at the priest with tear-stained eyes and sobbed, "You're in the church if I need you? Did you ever hear of a saint hiding in the church?"

The same may be said of friends who couldn't look beyond their spiritual studies in order to empathize with the hurting soul of a fellow seeker. I'm glad that doctorate degree in Religious Studies came in so handy when dealing with a mere mortal such as me. At least Karl Malden learned his lesson by the end of the film when he descended into the belly of a cargo ship where another murdered body laid. Thundering up to the top deck where the mob boss stood, being pelted with rocks, cans and rotted fruit, he proclaimed, "**This** is my parish." And turning to look the courageous workmen in the eye he said, "I'll stand by you to the end." He then lit a cigarette and was raised up out of the ship's hole on a cargo platform, showing in dramatic fashion the example of one rising to meet his own mission. At least he got it. Many do not.

How do you see yourself as a friend?

Do the actions of your compatriots make you uncomfortable? Are you able to see beyond their anger, their hurt, their self-destructive ways and actually accept them as created human beings with intrinsic value? If for no other reason than because their creator valued them first?

And by the writing of this, I am committing the very same sin -- I have abdicated this same friendship without knowing or understanding their personal circumstances. Maybe they were devastated by some horrible, tragic set of events. Maybe they have gone through their own crisis of faith and belief. Maybe they're just tired, as I was, and just needed a break. I, too, am judging our loss of friendship based on something they have or have not done without obtaining the full story.

And, just as equally, I am wrong.

So, I will value them as people in their own right and accept our distant circumstances as just that: a set of destiny's circumstances into which I have neither insight nor understanding. I miss them and wish them the best this world has to offer and beyond. Maybe, one day, we will meet up again. Maybe then we will find new ways to laugh, love and embrace each other's lives.

Can you do the same?

For me?

  For yourself?

    For your friends?

"Greater love has no one than this, that he lay down his life for his friends."
    -- John 15:13

Chapter 16
LOOKING FOR LOVE

"Let your ambition be to let your beloved see you clearly, your fears, your hopes, your scars, your dreams, your joy, your sorrow, your desires, your passions and your innermost life. This is giving the gift of self. If you do not give this gift, what is the use of giving any other?"

– The Couples Tao Te Ching

I glanced out the corner of my eye in order to catch a quick, fleeting look. My breath took a jolt. She's looking my way! Did she see me looking at her? Does she think I'm weird? What should I do? I can't just put my book down and run away. I'll have to pretend to keep reading and hope she doesn't notice again. I hope the teacher didn't see! Then I might get into trouble. Then we'd be kept after class for being disruptive, and then how would I explain to my parents their seven-year-old son was caught looking at a girl in his first-grade reading class?

She was sitting next to me on a low-built wooden chair, her legs crossed, wearing a red and black plaid dress, her white slip barely showing an inch beneath the hemline. Her red knee socks and black tennis shoes betrayed a tom-boy character common to many girls her age.

Sitting next to us was our teacher, Mrs. Pentell, wearing a stylish powder blue dress, black pumps and silver-framed glasses to match her silver ladies wristwatch. I was a devilish rogue myself, outfitted with a flat-top butch hair cut, cotton shirt and pants with white socks and tan, brush suede Hush Puppy shoes. Who could have resisted the lopsided grin of one such as I, with a missing front tooth and devil-may-care attitude?

She could.

Her haughty I-couldn't-care-less look was followed by a toss of hair and a swing of her young hips straight out the door. Without so much as a courteous acknowledgment of my attention or flattery-will-get-you-everywhere gesture, she ran off to the monkey bars, giggling with her girlfriends about some strange boy in reading class.

That's okay. I could handle it. After all, she was my first love.

Thirty-five years, five kids between us and separated by several lifetimes later, we found each other on a fluke. Thinking love may indeed blossom with the emotional awakening of those tender young years, we were married. We soon discovered that the devil-may-care attitude from first grade had become a permanent part of my personality, and her haughty I-couldn't-care-less posture had also ingrained itself into a fixed position of immutable durability. The suede Hush Puppies and red knee socks could not be salvaged.

Some Hollywood marriages have lasted longer. Ours came to a mutually thankful quick end.

Maybe love doesn't begin in the first grade. Maybe love can't jump decades to reclaim Cupid's intended arrow for two people. Maybe love was something I could only find in the books I came to cherish in reading class, beginning with Old Yeller and Black Beauty. Maybe love was just as much a fantasy as what was found between pages from authors with wild imaginations and wishful dreams of their own.

Yet, here I am today ready to tell you about love.

Right now my good friend Mike Duffy would say with overstated emphasis, "Whoa, whoa, whoa," as if to shout to the world: the LAST person you want telling you about love is THIS guy! And he would be right. I am the last person on this Earth who is in any position to talk about, let alone, expound on and illuminate, this thrill-a-minute called love. Having said that, I'm going to anyway. I can, because like a lonely, determined fisherman who keeps punishing himself day after day, putting his boat into the water, baiting his hook with brightly-colored spinning and whirling baits in hopes of landing the big one, I, too, have sought the elusive dream called love. Like the fisherman, it's been frustrating, demoralizing and, many times, appeared to be a futile exercise of human nature. It just wasn't to be found. Like the country song from the Urban Cowboy sound track, I felt like I was "looking for love in all the wrong places."

At this time, however, I feel I am in the fifth stage of understanding love, much like the fifth in the stages of wine tasting which are to see, swirl, smell, sip, savor and summarize. I've experienced the first four with very little harm and very thorough evaluation. Now I believe I am able to savor the components of love and, one day, may even be able to summarize how all this is supposed to work.

To begin, I realize I had a very misconstrued perspective on what love was supposed to be. To be truthful, I didn't know what love was supposed to look like, feel like or result from. The word was ambiguous to me, cloudy and murky. "I love you" was something you said to your mother because that was where your next meal and a clean pile of clothes were coming from. But what did it mean if you were to say it to someone else?

There are some who never get the concept of love. They go through life watching their back or not even venturing into this tumultuous arena of emotion because either: a) they were burned once or twice before; or b) they were too afraid to even try for fear they MIGHT get hurt. One author went so far as to say there are only three types of people: those that are out to screw you and tell you beforehand, those that are out to screw you but don't tell you beforehand, and those people that end up screwing you without intending to, but do so anyway. That's a tough way to live, and I knew that wasn't what I was looking for.

> "To love is to be vulnerable. Love anything, and your heart will certainly be wrung and possibly broken. If you want to make sure of keeping it intact, you must give it to no one, not even to an animal. Wrap it carefully around hobbies and little luxuries; avoid all entanglements; lock it up safe in the casket or coffin of your selfishness. But in that casket -- safe, dark, motionless, airless -- it will change. It will not be broken; it will become unbreakable, impenetrable, irredeemable."
> – C.S. Lewis

My difficulty in this area of finding love is exacerbated by the fact that I really like women. I like the way they laugh, the way they smell (Victoria's Secret Amber Romance Silkening Body Lotion is the best). I like the smiles that leave you wistful and weak, eyes that are playful and inviting. Size and structure are inconsequential--they all appeal to me because from my earliest times, women were all that surrounded me. I was raised by my loving and dutiful mother while my dad worked the second shift in a factory some 70 miles away. I was enveloped and attended to by grandmothers, aunts, cousins and friends, all women.

Here I am, baking in the kitchen as a youngster, streaks of flour and butter crisscrossing my freckled face, while the ladies yacked away about life, men, neighbors and, of course, other church ladies. The 80-year-old women flirted unashamedly as if they were 16 again, telling me how handsome I was and wishing they could take a generation or two from their age. I laughed and giggled right along with them as we played cards and checkers around the dining room table, my feet swinging from the chair, not yet grown enough to touch the floor. My 70-year-old aunt taught me the game of chess and marveled at my quick mastery of its nuances. One grandmother took me to the library while another patiently taught me how to play the piano and organ, recitals forever being my nemesis. I played tennis and swam and frolicked with female cousins.

I hate to admit this, but I've even put on one of those billowy, blowing hair dryer plastic bonnet contraptions with the three-foot hose attached as if it were an alien brain transference machine--all to fit in with the ladies! Mel Gibson didn't have to become electrocuted in a bathtub in the movie What Women Want to find out what women were thinking. Just ask me! I was one of them!

I was living in a world where the only guys I saw, and it wasn't that often, were my dad on the weekends as he came from the basement every now and then, and some classmates in school. But my most complex and intimate interactions were all with women. So is it any wonder I like them and relate to them better?

To me, women are like chocolate. Some are rich, dark and sinful like a strong selected morsel of Godiva. Can't have too many of those or you'll self-destruct in over-indulgence! Some are the more common milk chocolate you can find in abundance, consumed with regularity, but not wholly satisfying. Like chocolate delights, they come in so many different forms: bars, nibbles, cakes, pudding, as an accent surrounding a lovely dish or as a complementary covering such as chocolate-covered cherries with something sweet and delicious waiting inside.

With an understanding of the tangled variances and labyrinthine uniqueness of femaleness, one couldn't help but be expected to look for and find love with relative ease. I remember the first time I lost my heart (first-grade reading class), first full crush (me all of ten, she being a sixteen-year-old counselor at summer camp), first kiss I refused from a girl (me, a seventh grader; give me a break--I was scared!), first girlfriend, first real kiss, first love/lust and the inevitable first teacher fantasy (she taught junior high history wearing white go-go boots and a mini-skirt. How could you NOT fall for that!).

In many ways, these were not that different from my other firsts: my first job, my first car, my first weeks away from home at college. Interesting. Exciting certainly. Compelling. But I wasn't very confident of my abilities and very unsure at how things were suppose to progress from a haltering first start. Once, my dad picked me and my date up after a basketball game in order to take us home. With the very best manners of a properly trained gentleman's gentleman (think of Mr. French from the television show Family Affair), I opened the back door for my date to get in. As she slid over to allow me to follow her for an assumed brief moment of secretive hand-holding, I promptly shut the door and, to my dad's amazement, jumped into the passenger side of the FRONT seat so that I could work the gear shift on our new manual transmission car! Love doesn't get any more grand than that!

Other forms of advice didn't sink in or give any more insight than my own stumbling, bumbling ways. My dad's version of "the talk" was to one day, unannounced, leave a book on my bed entitled, The Way of a Man with a Maid. I had to assume that since we didn't have any servant's quarters, the maid part in this 1950 classic outlining instructions for the proper approach and conquering of the female gender, was a substitute for women.

I'm still not sure.

As an adult, another friend, commenting on my dating partner, advised, "I can see why you like her. But she'll drain you dry. There isn't enough money in the world to satisfy her."

And it turned out to be true. Another lesson learned, this one in love and finances.

For me, trying to be in love was like being thrown into debtor's prison. In 18th century London, a debtor's prison was where you were placed if you couldn't pay your bills. You had no money. AND, in addition to your original debt, for each day of your imprisonment, you were obligated for the expense of detaining you! The tourists would come by just to see what prisoner that day would be chosen to beg in the streets for release money.

Humiliation. Embarrassment. Shame.

I was constantly being put into a relationship "prison" that required something I did have -- love. And in addition, for every day I was in that relationship, I was being asked for more of what I was looking for to begin with! I, too, had my spectators who lined up to gawk and take pleasure at my ineptness. For me, the results were the same had I run out money in London: humiliation, embarrassment and shame.

After bumping along, falling in and out of what I thought to be love or something like it, I found I had been involved with a musician, a pilot, a sales rep, a teacher, a customer service rep, a clerk of courts, a business owner, and several other categories of talents, skills and professional careers. It had all culminated with two failed marriages, one of which was termed a "mail-order bride" by some of my more enlightened compadres who said that long distance failure was seen coming a long way off.

What can I say? This is a list of how not to go about finding that elusive, slippery, ornery, irritating, presumptuous thing called love. My theme song lyrics had become, "You give your hand to me and then you said 'Hello.' And I can hardly speak, my heart is beating so. And anyone can tell you think you know me well, but you don't know me."

For years, I felt like I was being tripped up by an ancient form of mutilation the Chinese practiced on their young girls called "footbinding." Between the ages of three and eight, and only according to astrological guidance as to the precise time, mothers would bind the feet of their little girls with sticky rice paste wrapping cloths, bending the toes until they literally grew UNDER the foot causing inflammation, prickling pain and numbing torture. This same procedure was used by ancients to preserve their mummies for all eternity!

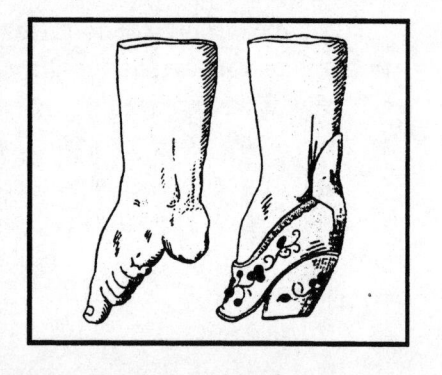

All this, turning their little girls' feet blue, yellow and swelling, dripping with pus, to succumb to the cultural quasi-fetishism goal of developing the rare "Golden Lotus," a foot measuring a total of THREE INCHES! This rite of passage through excruciating pain was promised to make the girl more beautiful so she could marry into a rich family where she wouldn't have to walk but, for the remainder of her life, be carried in a sedan chair. In *Becoming Madame Mao,* the main character ripped off her constraining wrapping in defiance of this perverted practice and ran away from not only her arranged marriage but her arranged life, calling her newly freed appendages "liberation feet."

That was me! Crippled and hobbled by a misunderstanding of love and what meaning it was suppose to have in one's life. It wasn't until I saw what this mangled mess of cloth and paste was doing to my feet that I could begin to understand the wonderful freedom that comes from running away from the child-like torture of misperceptions and misunderstandings. What I needed were liberation feet, a way in which to run a full race as a healthy, emotionally functional adult. But as an old man once told me while sitting at the counter in a local diner in Snohomish, Washington, "Everything itches when you can't move."

And I couldn't move. Couldn't budge an inch toward a healthier, more profound understanding of this most basic of all human emotions; the itch, not releasing its anguished captive.

An ancient Chinese saying is, "The more you try to please people--the more you will become their prisoner." I had become a prisoner of the expectations of all others except my own heart. The expectations of a son, a business professional, a church official, a public figure, a husband and more had all conspired to make me into someone not of my choosing or, worse, not of my being. As the title character of Josephine Hart's Damage reveals, "There is an internal landscape, a geography of the soul; we search for its outlines all our lives. And in my own life, I have traveled far, acquiring loved and unfamiliar companions ... I hid the awkwardness and pain with which I inclined towards my chosen outline, and tried to be what those I loved expected me to be."

It was in the midst of this turmoil and perplexity of mind and spirit . . . that I saw love.

I saw it in a waiting room over three days as a visitor to St. Mary's Hospital. I saw love in its myriad forms and fashion. I saw love in joy, sorrow, apprehension, exhaustion, intentness, suspicion, dedication, compassion, selflessness, worry, anger, resolve, resolution and gratitude. I saw love in strangers, family members, professionals and friends. I saw love in a way I had never seen nor experienced before.

Lou Cook is a dear friend and the mother of my friend, Kathy. Lou is what you'd expect in a loving and tender mother, but under her tender and genuine empathy for other people and their particular vicissitudes of life, is a hardened, steel plate of determination that has been molded by countless surgeries, health concerns, divorce, financial struggles, cancer and now this latest surprise. What was to have been an uncomplicated and fairly common angioplasty with a couple shunts put in her heart for better blood flow turned into a marathon of emotional upheaval. Word from the doctor was that her arteries were just too thin, too susceptible to collapse in a very short amount of time. The shunts would not hold. Triple bypass surgery was needed. Plans for going home to her own bed, her own food and her own family with renewed health and vigor changed to a gut-wrenching decision that literally encapsulated life and death. When she agreed to the surgery, it set into motion a chain of actions and reactions that, in their whole, constituted love in every respect.

Instead of going to a much-anticipated hockey game involving sorely missed children, time was devoted to the support of this wonderful woman and her family in their most difficult of circumstances. One sister called her brother, who immediately made arrangements to fly 1000 miles to be by his mother's side. At the end of the day, hugs were shared and tears would flow that would not stop for three days, appearing at the most unexpected moments. The next morning, Lou was prepped for the O.R. The surgeon displayed confidence in her health while the nurses patted our backs as we filed out of the room one-by-one, not knowing for sure if this was to be our last goodbye. No one said those words, but they were etched in every forehead, set in the stony stare of each family member, one to another.

The next five hours were pure, uninsulated hell as each did what they had to do to stay occupied, not wanting to think of what was happening at that very moment or what could tragically happen at any moment. One sister fills in her new address book, a gift from Christmas. Another reads a magazine, eyes glazing over the words and pictures, blurred by the incomprehensible thought, "I can't believe this is going on." Her husband watches television. And then the stories begin to flow. Each family member chiming in with anecdotes about their lives, their mother, their common experiences of bad dates, parental intrusion and what their own kids are going through.

Each time the elevator door opens, all heads turn and all eyes search for their brother. When he arrives, it's another round of hugs, kisses and, again, the tears. But now the family is complete. He brings pictures of his girls and personal messages created for their grandmother. Laughter builds with each story about their latest misadventures in Florida. People smile as they walk by, overhearing a snatched punch line that elicits a new round of chuckles. I sit back and watch this spectacle called a family, this unimaginable reveler called love. Through sorrow and anxious anticipation of good news or bad, there is a bond that nothing will break.

A nun walks by and says, "I notice you seem to be waiting a long time. Would you tell me what's happening with your family member?" She then kneels down in the center of this semi-circle of humans and says, "Someone will think I'm crazy for doing this, but, oh well. Let's pray." And this woman, a woman of God, exhorts the creator of Heaven and Earth to bring skill to the surgeons and health to the patient. She departs, her love left behind to encourage and comfort.

A stranger steps off the elevator, unknown to anyone waiting. After walking by several times, the stranger eventually stops and says, "And how is your loved one?" This stranger could see the pain and anxiousness, sense the dread and anticipation of a yet-undeclared verdict. He stopped and connected with words of a similar set of circumstances and good news that it will turn out well.

"Thank you," one sister says. We needed to hear that."

Word comes that the surgery went well, she is in recovery and all is expected to be fine. Relief and release. Pent-up fear and anguish come in the form of tears, smiles and holding of hands. I want to start high-fiving everyone in the room but don't feel that it's quite appropriate.

Later, standing next to her bed, tubes and monitoring apparatus coming out of every conceivable section of her body, she struggles, fighting her way through the fog of the anesthetic. It's a gruesome scene. You don't know if this is normal or the last gasp of life. The nurse says she's fine, but yet you wonder, and still no one leaves her side. If she struggles, we all will struggle with her and will see her through to her full awakening, on this side of the river of life or the next.

On the third day, we're again sitting in the waiting room. Long nights, long drives home, all for the cause and support of this dear mother. How much more is there left to give? It's hard to keep it all together as nerves are becoming frayed, emotions on the brink. Everyone is getting set to leave for the day when her husband says he'll say a bit longer. He says he wants to be the last because he just can't go, he just can't leave her behind. And the tears fall from his cheeks as the gates open for relief and the family surrounds him with hands on his shoulders, around his neck and quiet words of strength and understanding are shared.

The oldest sister continues to be a primary care-giver, but she, too, is coming to the end of her composure and steadfastness. She needs a break, and so I go out and buy her birthday present two weeks early. She needed something for herself. I found a unique tea kettle and an assortment of flavored teas of orange, cherry, blackberry and almond that she can make that night to soothe her own soul and give resolve a rest.

Birthdays are not just dates on a calendar. They are events in a person's life. In Mutant Message Down Under, the illustration of this comes from the Aborigine tribe. For them, celebration comes whenever a member of their tribe has come to the realization they have accomplished something, has turned a corner as a human, has made an internal advancement the rest of the tribe should know about. That's when they celebrate. That's their REAL birthday.

And so it is with Kathy. Her real birthday needed to be celebrated tonight. Quietly, she is handed a hot cup of tea from one who feels like HIS real birthday has also just occurred. I had become her personal "heart monitor."

> *"No matter what we achieve, if we don't spend the majority of our time with people we love and respect, we cannot possibly have a great life."*
> *– Jim Collins*

This is the meaning of love.

Love is being aware of everyone else around you. Aware of their personal needs. Aware of what you can do or not do that would have a positive or nourishing effect on their lives. Aware of pain and hurt, joy and jubilation, contributing and being a part of whatever is being felt at that moment without thought or concern for yourself.

Love is an active participant, not an idle bystander.

Love looks for ways to interject a word or a touch that

conveys acceptance and acknowledgment of someone else's experience. It validates feelings and passages. It might come from the word of a stranger or the prayer of a nun. Love might be found in the pat on the shoulder from a nurse or the heartfelt gaze of a doctor preparing someone for a monumental precipice.

Love is loyalty. Love is honesty. Love is simply there without recrimination or expectation.

Love frees you to be yourself. To give yourself. To express yourself in tears or laughter without thought or internal editing. Love does not hold back for fear of judgment.

This is the gift of love.

This is life as it should be lived.

And this is what I've been looking for.

Chapter 17
TERRORISM ON THE HOME FRONT

"When I looked around me at all that was done in the name of religion, I was horrified."
-- Lyof N. Tolstoi

Are you a terrorist?

Of course you're not. How could I even dare to ask such a repugnant question of you? And certainly not a terrorist as we think of those who have committed such atrocities as the World Trade Towers tragedy of September 11, 2001. **They** are terrorists. **They** unilaterally destroyed families and lives and created gut-wrenching havoc that will be felt for generations. **They** are the ones who need a lesson in true justice and the unavoidable consequence of retribution for their actions.

They are the terrorists.

But are they the **only** terrorists?

Could we even fathom the thought that we may be terrorists too?

Let's take a look.

▼ Terrorists think only of the point they want to make without regard for the devastation it may cause.

▼ Terrorists justify their destructive behavior as a necessary means to achieve their desired goals.

▼ Terrorists use the facade of moral and religious principle to cover their evil nature and intent.

▼ Terrorists create insidious devastation that compounds the resulting scars and nightmares.

▼ Terrorists often appear to be innocent, normal human beings while masking a deceptive and nefarious spirit.

▼ Terrorists don't give their victims a choice.

▼ Terrorists plan their deeds in secret. They do not want to come under scrutiny for fear of being exposed.

▼ Terrorists do not recognize or abide by good faith.

▼ Terrorists refuse to acquiesce to the common laws of humanity such as compassion, mercy and the Golden Rule: "Do unto others as you would have them do unto you."

▼ Terrorists reject the judicial laws of their own society when they do not fit their needs.

▼ Terrorists must use physical force to achieve their fervent results.

▼ Terrorists hide behind smiles and a thin layer of civility to the general populace while underneath they work their destructive plans to their own timing.

▼ Terrorists have concentric circles of impact beyond the original victim. Collateral damage is not only accepted, it is an unacknowledged added victory.

▼ Terrorists do not use acceptable logic or reasonable lines of thinking.

▼ Terrorists do not think or feel as normal people do. They lack conscience, guilt and empathy for other humans.

▼ Terrorists do not feel the pain and suffering of other people. The aftermath of victory is all that matters in their warped and perverted minds.

▼ When accused, terrorists scream their "rights" are being violated.

▼ Terrorists use truth to protect their lies, and lies are upheld as the absolute truth.

▼ Terrorists have an inverted world where they see nothing wrong with their actions and, from their point of view, their perverted world of hurt and anger is the correct and proper world.

▼ Terrorists say, "Do not oppose us by our own methods and means. For then **you** are the one who is violating your own code of civility."

▼ Terrorists use a false display of amiability as a weapon and wear it as a suit of armor saying, "**We** are the normal ones. **They**, the accusers, are the ones acting irrationally."

▼ Terrorists like the results of fear, anxiousness and intimidation.

▼ Terrorists want you to change **Your** life to comply with theirs.

▼ Terrorists want to control and manipulate the circumstances to their exclusive benefit.

▼ Terrorists want their victims to feel that everything is alright when, in fact, the victims feel something is terribly wrong, but are not quite sure why.

The victims of terrorists feel trapped without options or hope of escape. The victims don't know what to do or how to deal with the circumstance forced upon them. They can only live moment-to-moment.

Victims of terrorists feel compelled to perform acts contrary to their inclinations. They may even take on an empathy for their captors.

Victims need to re-construct what is "normal" to achieve correct patterns of thought and conduct.

Haunting memories may linger. And it will take a number of outside influences to rescue them.

▼ Terrorists point fingers at what others are doing wrong without addressing their own violations.

▼ Terrorists do not view themselves as being dangerous or destructive.

▼ Terrorists feel a nobility in their actions -- even a righteous obligation.

▼ Terrorists feel vindicated in their cause and will fight to the death against all who oppose them and their view.

- ▼ The law protects the terrorists as long as the law only sees their outward compliance to conformity.

- ▼ Terrorists parade their victims in full view to show that all is well-- what have they done wrong?

- ▼ Terrorists do not acknowledge the fruit of their actions.

- ▼ Terrorists are most secure when they feel unaffected by the real, outside world. However, if this real world contradicts their being, terrorists retaliate until once again they feel left alone.

Control and retaliation are the code words of the terrorist's manifesto.

We, of course, are not terrorists.

Unless . . .

We have used physical force to get our own way.

Have lied to gain an advantage.

Have hidden in a cloak of smiles and civil banter only to be plotting a different plan of attack.

Have used guilt and emotional blackmail to advance our goals.

Have held down the weaker--using our position to harness others within the iron-grip of our control.

Have given no choice but to follow our commands or be pummeled with our scathing wrath.

When every day is a battle.

When you will fight to the death for your gain.

When there is no other world than your own.

That is when you might stop.

Reconsider your position.

Assess what your actions may be doing to another party.

Is pain your true goal?

Could there be a better way when considering all involved, including yourself?

You may wish to find another way.

> You might try a different solution.

Just one more time.

> For fear
>
> you may be
>
> a terrorist.

Chapter 18
THE QUESTION

If God were to come to Earth next Sunday morning, whose church service would He attend?

Whose choir, that worked for weeks to achieve just the right pitch, tempo and harmony, would He hear?

Whose new set of clothes would He see?

Whose hymnal would He sing from? Would it be the traditional hardcover songs of glory with the gold embossed church name on the front that took six months of bake sales and three Sundays of pleading from the minister in order to raise the necessary funds, or the spiral-bound soft cover edition at $2.99?

Whose parking lot, where trustees work so hard to patch and paint to be sure no one goes outside the lines, would He park in? And would He park inside the lines?

Whose pew would He sit in? The hard oak bench with the scuffing and scratch marks from a thousand sets of black sole shoes or the soft folding chairs with 2-inch foam padding and brightly colored fabric?

With whose communion service would He feel most involved? The one with bland, unsalted crackers and grape juice, tiny cubes of white bread and Kool-Aid or thin, punctured wafers with tart, red wine?

Whose sermon would stir His heart? The one with many homilies, metaphors and deep doctrinal themes, the quiet readings from the monotoned octogenarian wearing a tight white collar or the energetic, rookie assistant pastor who doubles as the bass player in the youth group band and makes a lot of analogies to current movies and music?

Whose reading of Scripture would be endearing to Him? The booming voice of the baritone deacon trained in public vibrato? The small, halting utterance of the frightened grade school child reading the Good Book out loud for the very first time? Or the soft, injured whisper of the battered wife, each prophetic revelation a public confession of shame, which always resulted in someone asking the usher to "pleeeeaaasssse" turn the sound system higher so you can hear the woman? If she is going to read, you may as well be able to hear her, for goodness' sake.

Whose offering would He most appreciate? The one collected in a round, wooden platter with the soft, green-felt bottom, the beige cardboard bucket that looks like a freshly washed logo-less container from KFC or the fancy, royal blue bag with the long solid oak handles where you don't have to pass it to one another but just reach out and drop in your money? Would He reject the quarter your mom gave you to put in the offering plate because it didn't really come from you?

Would He give a knowing, inside nod to the check for $5,000 that was designated for use in replacing the lighting in the fellowship hall?

Would He look up and see your vaulted ceilings with tongue-and-groove varnished panels with the silent rotating fans attached to draw the heat up and away on those sultry summer mornings?

Would He notice those brightly colored banners that hang between each window that proclaim the attributes of Love, Peace, Long-suffering, Kindness and Forgiveness that took so many painstaking hours of cutting and gluing of cloth and glitter and then still needed final approval for placement from the council of elders?

Whose organ would He relish? Whose piano would delight? Whose robes would give the proper air of authority and power? Whose pulpit would give the most appropriate setting? Whose cross would He gaze upon?

Whose congregation, gathering or flock of worshippers would He most like to spend time with afterwards? Whose Sunday dinner would He eat? On whose couch would He take a nap?

Maybe He wouldn't go to a church at all. Maybe He would choose a synagogue on a Friday night or a grass hut, tent or cave. Maybe He would sit by a pool, stand on a hill, walk in the street or lie down on a bed. Maybe He would cover His head, light a candle, hum a few bars or quietly be still. Maybe He wished it were Saturday night or later in the day or that Sunday only came once a month or at most twice a year.

Maybe . . . .

If God were to come to earth next Sunday morning, whose church service would He attend?

It's just a question.

        Why does it make you so uncomfortable?

Chapter 19
DELIVERANCE FROM DISAPPOINTMENT

"If you can't fly, run. If you can't run, walk. If you can't walk, crawl, but by all means keep moving."
— Martin Luther King Jr.

December 24th, 9:10 a.m.

I felt happy, giddy almost. That's how I get when I know I'm going to see my kids. After being divorced for 12 years, seeing my kids has always made me ecstatic. I love being with them, talking with them and hearing all their stories about school, their friends and what they have been up to. I live four hours south of them and had driven up the day before in order to purchase their gifts, buy all the wrapping paper and scotch tape, plan where we would eat our dinner, and maybe scope out a church service in which to spend an hour singing songs of the season together. Things really couldn't be much better, unless I lived closer, of course. But all-in-all, this was going to be a great Christmas.

I picked up the telephone and called my ex-wife to set a time to pick up the kids that day for our holiday together. I had expected them to be ready in an hour or two, which would leave just enough time to put the finishing bows, ribbons and name tags on each present. It had been a rocky road for my ex-wife and me. We had differing views on how much time the kids and I would get to spend together, and it caused a continuous riff over schedules, timing and activities. But this was Christmas. I was coming on my exact day at the exact time she would prescribe, and the kids and I would have a wonderful day of laughing, eating, movies and horseplay.

The first gifts I ever received from my kids remain, today, close at hand: a golf counter from my son Donny, a *Matchbox Twenty* C.D. from Trevor, a pen and pencil set from my daughter Stacy. These are daily reminders of how innocently marvelous kids are in presenting those first gifts they hope the recipient will enjoy and, in contrast, how difficult it must be to live under the burdensome circumstances in which we find ourselves today. I think of Christmases when I was their age. They were not fraught with emotional struggles involving feuding parents, disputed pick-up times and pejorative questions such as, "Where are you going to be?" and "Don't bring anything home that came from HIM, understand?" The paramount concern was universal: When are we going to open the presents? We would go to one grandma's house for dinner and gifts on Christmas Eve. Christmas morning we exchanged presents at home and then traveled for dinner to the other grandparents' house for another round of the same. Not a bad arrangement and very typical in my neighborhood.

But my children, and many others of their generation, are making sure they don't upset one parent over the other, don't show any type of favoritism between the adults, and certainly don't talk about the plans being made with Mom or Dad. I have read countless books on how to help your children through divorce and, yet, the exact same problems crop up time after time. One parent or the other establishes a preference, the other stands up for their "rights" and the kids are left in the swirling turmoil of "what about us?"

But this Christmas will be different. I can feel it. After all, I just talked to her a few days before. She said that everything was set and to call that morning to see when the kids would be ready.

And so I called, 9:10 a.m. on December 24th, Christmas Eve, ready for a reuniting of father and children.

After a brief exchange of civility and some hemming and hawing around, it was finally admitted that in the 48 hours since our last conversation, she had made other plans for that day--the kids were going to the movies with her parents. There would be no Christmas for me and the kids this year.

None. Zip. Zero. Nada.

"This is what you deserve," she would say and no amount of pleading, begging or bargaining on my part would sway her position.

But this was MY day! How could this be happening when everything had been planned and agreed to, not just a few days ago, but recorded in court documents and judges' decrees from a decade ago? I tried to arrange a lunch, a breakfast, any time where I could give them their gifts, see them and tell them how much I missed and loved them. But the forces in control that day stayed in control, and it was not to be.

My mind screamed in agony. Revenge would only be satisfactory if it included chains, insects and a hot desert sun at noon. Since none of these were available in Wisconsin during the winter holiday season, I was left with a bottomless crater of inconsolable disappointment.

The titanic crash just heard was my heart.

Sadness.

Despair.

A tear falls as I place the phone down and slump into a wicker rocker, their gifts, still unwrapped and sitting in a plastic bag, at my feet. It's not the music or trinkets that matter. It's not being able to see the happiness that comes from giving a gift, showing someone you care deeply about that you were thinking of him and want to bring him joy. I could use these gifts some other time, but it wouldn't be the same. THIS time they were meant for today. I would now be retracing my steps back to the store, returning a favorite C.D. for each of the boys, a selection of beaded bracelets in a decorative wire basket for Stacy. Also returned would be the unopened wrapping paper and tape purchased to make their gifts look pretty and alluring. I thought about the things I had planned to say to the kids personally since we get so little face time nowadays. But those gifts, too, would go unopened, unsaid.

Those had been my plans.

What do you do with disappointment, the despondency and frustration that comes when your plans do not turn out as you had hoped with such fervor and expectation? What do you do with the pain and unfairness of creating a good and right and normal activity, and still your honorable intentions are shut out? It's as if the massive doors of a giant castle that contained your highest hopes and dreams were closed and locked in your face. You stand forlorn and trembling, not knowing exactly what to do.

There is a saying posted on my office wall: "Difficulty is the excuse history never accepts." So am I suppose to dig in, stand firm and re-trench to do battle? What would that accomplish? Who was the one **truly** being tested here? My kids? No, they're just trying to survive and get through this morass of adult stupidity. My ex-wife? No, she was using the advantage of possession being 9/10ths of the law and would simply not relinquish it. Who was really being put to the test?

It was me. Now what was I going to do?

I found myself in a similar situation when I was flying home from a speaking engagement. It was an evening flight filled with numerous other weary business travelers anxious to get home. I began to read a brand new, just-purchased book when a flight attendant pushed her cart past my aisle seat in order to begin pouring drinks for the passenger just ahead. As she reached around the cart to pour a cup of water, she misjudged the direction of the bottle and water streamed away from her intended target, over the plastic lip of the cup and onto the pages of my book below. So much water had poured out I had to tilt my book upright and let the river flow down the pages, leaving wet droplets to form in my lap and around my feet. I glared at her with silent disgust and contempt, as if to say, "I can't believe you just did that!" Her surly attitude matched mine with, "Sorry, it's a bit bumpy," when, in fact, it was one of the smoother flights of my career, no bumpier than sitting in your own living room lounger.

I mopped and patted the water with a couple napkins tossed my way and watched in horror as, right before my eyes, the pages began to curl. My brand new book with its anointed words were shriveling up like the wicked witch of the west crying, "I'm melting! I'm melting!" I value my books, and I had highlighted portions of this particular text that had special meaning to me. Now they appeared ruined.

I finished cleaning up and continued to read, but every few chapters, I turned back to look at the pinched and now withered pages. I could still read them, I could still see my highlights-- they just were not in their original, perfect form. All the value, content and essence were still there. Even today, it's still there--even as I continue to turn the curled and atrophied pages.

So are my feelings, relationship, and commitment to my kids. Yes, I got dumped on with a bucket full of retribution that derailed my anticipated event. But everything still survived and remained intact: all my love, all my commitment, all my devotion, just not in its perfect form. So the question remained --what was I going to do now?

When facing disappointment, choices were available to me then as they are for each of us today. It doesn't matter if it's disappointment over a missed job promotion, a forgotten appointment with a spouse, a lower-than-expected grade in school, a lost possession or being stood up and/or embarrassed by someone we know. It feels the same with varying degrees of failure, unfulfillment, discouragement, and a sense of obstructive impedance. We've been stopped from doing what we wish or possessing what we wish to have.

What are we to do?

We can pound our fists on the unmovable, steel doors of the castle until our knuckles are bloody and broken. With each strike of frustration and anger, we can scream, "Let me in! I only came to love you! I brought gifts specifically chosen with you in mind! Why is this happening? Please let me in!" And finally, after hours or days or weeks (or, for some, a lifetime) of fruitless banging and crashing, we slump at the base of the door, our shoulders propped against the impenetrable obstacle that stands in the way of our plans, our dreams, our hopes, and we give up.

"I GIVE UP!" you shout to no one in particular.

"You don't want my gifts and time and effort. FINE. Then I just give up." Where once generosity and compassion filled your heart, now hatred has turned sickly rancid. The acid bitterness has created your own impervious fortress of callous contempt.

You've chosen to give up.

Some may choose to give up on themselves and the caustic bitterness is turned inward. Confidence that flourished because you were giving something of value has turned to crushing feelings of little or no self-worth. No one wants what you have to give. Fine. Then I also give up on myself. Fredrick Buechner, says a "life you clutch, hoard, guard, and play safe with is in the end a life worth little to anybody, including yourself." But that was our choice.

It all comes down to choices. Every corner we turn and every breath we inhale are made of the imperceptible microbes of choices. Adding to the complexity of this situation is the fact that NOTHING is harder than having to make a choice at the lowest, most despondent time of your life. You don't FEEL like making a choice. What you FEEL like doing is procuring the largest, loudest, most destructive cannon you can find. You FEEL like stuffing its gaping mouth with the blackest, most explosive gun powder followed by a massive cannonball. trike the fuse with a hot corrosive match snapped off your belt buckle and let that sucker blow! POW! The earth shattering collision of your all-powerful force smashing through that unsuspecting and formerly impassable castle door will show everyone who's really the boss! That's what you FEEL like doing.

Force. Power. Strength.

The reality is you CAN choose to do that. Instead of a cannon as your weapon, you choose a lawyer, a court suit or maybe your physical presence in a place where you're not wanted. our gunpowder and cannonball are the acrimonious words you spew in your outrage, hoping they will tear apart any shred of resistance Then you can triumphantly stride through the dangling, battered door and claim your prize.

You CAN do that.

We all have.

It's what we WANT to do.

But what remains after that choice? The once fragile relationship to the hindering obstacle is now shattered beyond any repair. The prize has been taken by force. The victory is shallow. You got what you wanted. our plans, your wishes are now recognized and complied with in reluctance and fear. But you've WON! Congratulations! Throw yourself a party. And by the way--pour only ONE glass of champagne because no one else will be there to celebrate with you. The bubbles that temporarily tickle your nose will shortly dissipate. The glass will soon be empty.

Philip Yancy said, "Love can never be forced. It flows out of fullness, not fear."

Anything obtained by force and fear is not capable of lasting. Alexander the Great built the world's largest empire by rampaging through country after country. Strength, power and might overcame any and all obstructions. However, ONE YEAR after his death at age 30, his empire fell apart. His selfish and proud generals succumbed to infighting and disputes over conquered territories. Everything Alexander the Great had attained through force was gone. It didn't last. It couldn't.

Force and fear are certainly weapons to achieve your goals. But, eventually, when you get squeezed--what's inside comes out.

A Chinese proverb says:

If you want to be happy for one hour - take a nap.
If you want to be happy for one day - go fishing.
If you want to be happy for one month - get married.
If you want to be happy for one year - inherit a lot of money.
If you want to be happy for life - help others.

I wanted to be happy for a lifetime, so I chose to do something for my kids, to help them in some way that involved a different type of force, a force that required as much strength and determination of will as any soldier suiting up for war. Except this form of force derived its strength from resolve--resolve through love.

> **"I graduated from the finest school, the love between parent and child. In this school you learn the measure not of power, but of love; not of victory, but of grace; not of triumph, but of forgiveness."**
> **–Mark Helprin**

David Eggers, in his book *A Heartbreaking Work of Staggering Genius,* said he never knew anything about his father, never knew anything outside of what he and his siblings had seen for themselves. He said he wanted to know what his father thought about him, what his father's feelings were about who they had become and how they had turned out.

I decided I wanted my kids to know how I felt about them outside of their own observations. I would put together a scrapbook. I would use my time, when during this holiday season we should have been physically closer to each other, to draw my heart to theirs through pictures and words. I gathered up years and years of history in hundreds of snapshots taken from the time they were born to their present age. I organized this pictorial journey chronologically, pausing along the way to refresh their memories with letters and cards, both given to me by them as children and my correspondence of encouragement in return. Each child will have their own personal record of a life with their dad.

I was making a choice to love, to redeem time for eternity. The ancient Chinese say that "love contains the power of a thousand suns. It's beauty radiates a transforming energy that enlivens all who see it." I wanted my kids to be transformed by seeing a greater goodness rather than torn apart by acrimonious selfishness. There will come a place for us to be together without interference or emotional hindrances. But rather than thrashing myself against an obstinate door, I will step back and instead take resolve.

* I will resolve to keep loving you even if you cannot receive my love.

* I will resolve to show you gifts of kindness and generosity of spirit.

* I will resolve to be patient and wait.

* I will resolve to be here, at the door, when you need help at any time in your life.

* I will resolve to be here a hundred years from now, because God has promised me that you, my children, will know I love you.

It's been said, "Never try to teach a pig to sing. It only wastes your time and it annoys the pig." I think I'll tie a noose around this hog and take it for a walk.

It's a terrible and disturbing paradox of life.

I cannot learn unconditional love without having love taken away.

"Paradoxes cannot be solved as problems are solved. They can only be accepted and cherished."

I cannot partake in the joy of kindness without knowing the unkind treatment from others.

"But this intimate experience in which every bit of life is touched by a bit of death can point us beyond the limits of our existence. It can do so by making us look forward in expectation to the day when our hearts will be filled with perfect joy, a joy that no one shall take away from us."
– Henri Nouwen

I cannot obtain perseverance without having to endure unpleasantness.

True gratitude for a life given comes from experiencing the pain of having a portion of your life taken away.

This Christmas, I'll think about you, my children.

I'll miss you and I'll hurt tremendously.

I will also look forward to the day when God's promise to me is fulfilled.

Disappointment is not
my enemy.

Disappointment is my reminder that all of life is a choice.

And I choose to love.

Chapter 20
LOST

"Love your enemies just in case your friends turn out to be a bunch of bastards."
– R.A. Dickson

I consider myself a pretty open-minded person: open to new ideas, new experiences, new friendships. I've had the opportunity to travel throughout a number of different countries while working for Crime Stoppers International, both teaching and as a guest. I've had an exchange student from Senegal in Western Africa live at my house for a month--the first place away from home at which he had ever stayed, after landing just two hours before at O'Hare International Airport. It was an amazing evening as we sat on my front porch, the sky gradually turning from iridescent pink to streaks of orange and red to, finally, midnight blue and starlit black, exchanging our stories of home and family in a combination of broken English phrases and flailing hand gestures. I saw my little corner of the world through his new-born eyes: America with its neatly mowed yards and single-family homes all lined up and ready for inspection.

I've delved into new and exotic cultures and customs whenever I travel. I always seek out the local restaurants in order to attain the real colloquial tastes and aromas as best I can. One of my most satisfying evenings was sharing drinks and conversation in Phoenix, Arizona with seven other people from such diverse backgrounds as South America, Japan, England, Australia and, of course, other Yanks. Fascinating stories. Fantastic adventures. It was all so wonderful--delightful to the ear and intellect.

But recently, I've had some uncomfortable feelings. I rankled at seeing a newspaper ad written in two languages side-by-side. I resented it when I heard about the struggles of teachers in our school system, trying to educate children who do not know the native tongue because their parents haven't learned it yet themselves. Businesses are forced to cater to this bilingual dilemma by offering multi-language employee manuals, greeting posters and menus.

As I said, I enjoy people from other cultures, but I have begun to ask myself, "Why haven't they learned to speak and read in English? I certainly wouldn't expect some other country to adapt to me if I were planning to live there. Why are we having to adapt to them?"

It was in this confusing, internal mix of thoughts and debate that I was shopping at a large discount store just before Christmas. As I rushed around the corner, intent on my destination of the men's department (yes--I am a typical male shopper: Seek/Find/Buy/Go), I tumbled over a small boy, maybe eight or nine years old. I pulled myself up short to keep from completely knocking him over, and quickly side-stepping the brown-haired youngster with a 360-degree move that would have made the highlight reel of SportsCenter had I been a power forward for the Milwaukee Bucks.

As I glanced back at the boy, I saw, by his dress and complexion, that he was of this other culture-- the one that was not learning what I had to learn or speaking the language I had been taught to speak. With a twinge of guilt, I was within an eyelash of thinking, but had not yet formulated the complete thought, "Why don't they even try to fit in?" when I saw tears, big wet pools of terror, not looking at me or our near collision, but at something beyond me, past me and farther along. He was urgently, intensely looking down each aisle, not outright crying or panicking, just turning his head, taking a few steps forward and then back, searching with wide, moist eyes.

Immediately I could tell he was lost. He gave a slight whimper, like a newborn pup, as he moved down the next row, quietly saying some form of "Mom? Mom?" as he went on.

You know the feeling, especially at that young, untested age. We've all experienced the sinking, desperate, drowning feeling of knowing you are lost. You're searching for a parent or friend who has become separated from you. Your heart pounds faster. Your mind is racing. You don't want to cry, but you're on the verge of bursting into uncontrollable sobs. You secretly say to yourself, "Where are you?"

I could see the feeling in his eyes. And I remembered being lost myself.

I was about his age. My parents had taken me to the Milwaukee Museum and, somehow, we had become separated in the old town section which depicted life from 100 years ago. The light was dim and, looking up into the sea of adult legs and bodies, I suddenly realized I didn't recognize any of the faces. It's then that moment of panic sets in and you wonder, what should I do? Will I ever find them again? I sat down on a wooden bench, all the while looking up and down the man-made street and waited, trying to stay calm, trying not to lose it. After what seemed an eternity, but was probably only a few minutes, my mom came walking by and I hurriedly grabbed her hand, relieved to have been found and safe once more.

Yes, I knew what it felt like to be lost. It crossed all boundaries of age and culture. In an instant, my prejudiced thoughts were replaced by the universal affection of camaraderie. We were both, in that moment, just little boys lost--him, looking for his mother, and me, another, bigger boy who had been there before and remembered what it was like.

"Have you lost your mom?" I asked.

"Ye, ye, ye, yes," he stammered, valiantly holding back the flood of tears he wanted so desperately to let go.

"Would you like me to help you find her?"

"Ye, ye, yes," nodding up and down with eager anticipation, not knowing what else to say to this gringo stranger.

"Follow me. We'll go to the front counter and have your mom paged over the intercom. I'm sure she'll be right up to get you." I turned and began walking, peering back every other step to be sure the little one was still following. I didn't have to worry. He no longer was looking from aisle to aisle. His eyes were still moist but glued directly to the middle of my back. He wasn't going to look anywhere else, he was following me to the promised land, the land of milk and honey and . . . his mom. Safety. Home.

We found her. A few brief minutes after the announcement, she came from an entirely different direction, pushing her cart of purchases and what looked to be his sister crammed into the riding seat. His eyes lit up. From 50 feet away he saw her and ran to his salvation. I heard the obligatory question that comes from the lexicon of all parents: "Where have you been?" And, again, all was right in his world.

I turned and began walking back to the men's department. I thought of how quickly, how immediately, I had identified with that frightened little boy once I knew he was lost. Without conscious reasoning or deliberate reflection, I instantly knew his feelings and fear. Pettiness had slipped away. I'm glad my heart could still empathize with his pain. I'm encouraged my cynicism had not built a barrier too high or insurmountable. I'm glad I could help.

Do you remember how you felt when you were lost? Can you feel the helplessness, the dismay, the concession to circumstances bent on your defeat?

Who helped you find your way home?

What will happen today if you meet someone in the same state of affairs? Maybe all he needs is a friendly smile and "Is there anything I can do?" When we're lost, just knowing there is one other person, even a stranger, who is turning their attention to our needs, makes us feel better, doesn't it?

Less alone. Less afraid. Someone else is using their eyes and ears and brain to make a plan that will bale us out.

They give us hope.

We all get lost.

We each need a helping hand, an encouraging word, a point in the right direction.

Today might be your day
to be someone's hero.

Epilogue

The purpose of sharing these thoughts was to talk to my kids. I am in the midst of a most difficult time. They were very young when their mother and I divorced. My time with them was reduced from being a father to a visitor every other weekend, with some extra days during the summer. Their own time with grandparents, cousins and other relatives was cut off. This was neither my choice nor theirs. But without the support of the judicial system for the role of father while not being married to their mother, there isn't much one can do to change the practical reality of the situation (thus, the reason for my book and seminar series, *A Divorced Dad's Guide To Seeing Your Kids: what judges, attorneys and your ex have not told you.*)

My kids and I have struggled through the past 12 years to stay connected, but the interference has become impenetrable. I have felt more and more disjointed in my relationship to them, and it breaks my heart. I kept looking ahead to that time in the future when we would be unfettered in our communication and we could know each other, as a dad, as friends . . . something . . . anything.

The more I thought about it, I came to realize that the future was not promised to me--or them. I had no idea if I would be alive another day, another week, let alone five years from now when they were in college or on their own. With the uncertainty of the future, I was left with a disheartened feeling of loss.

My friend--a dad--has a wonderful relationship with his son. They build rockets together, talk, go out for lunch and record music for each other. Most mornings, while on the way to the airport, this father would call his son on his cell phone just to say he loved him and have a great day. I told this father, "I know you value your relationship with your son. I know you love him beyond description. But you REALLY don't know what you have in this relationship, simply because you've never NOT had it. You don't know what it's like to have all the same feelings of love, devotion and care and not be able to share it with your child."

And that's the position I'm in. I love my children, Donny, Trevor and Stacy, and cannot communicate with them in an open and honest fashion due to circumstances that, at this time, surround their lives.

But I had to communicate with them somehow. Stephen King said, in his book *On Writing: A Memoir of the Craft*, that writing was really talking into the future. Somewhere in the future, my kids might read these chapters and really know how much I wanted to love and share with them right now. But now is not possible. By writing this, the future may still be.

This book was written as if I were sitting on my back deck or riding in the car with my kids. It's what I would have said if we had the opportunity. At least now, it's on paper.

Having read this, if you are not my kids, I welcome you. As stated in the introduction, we are all common sojourners. I know you have felt many of the same feelings, only under different circumstances. No matter our lot in life, we are all in this together. That's why these chapters rang true for you. It was like sitting in an airplane, overhearing a personal and intimate conversation between a parent and his child. You don't mean to listen, but you can't help it. That's okay. It's no secret to anyone who knows me how difficult it's been not to see and talk with my kids. It has torn my heart . . . I miss them so. But I am not alone, and so I am not afraid to share these lessons with you, however, with a purpose.

Truth cannot ultimately be hidden. If you know the truth and do not share it, someone else will. Truth has its own life and cannot be destroyed, ignored or twisted forever. Truth is like that gooey substance Silly Putty. No matter what you do to it, add or subtract from it, at the end of the day, it's still Silly Putty in its own essence, ready for another round of interaction, use and misuse.

I have found that once I know something to be true, it's imperative that I share it. By sharing it, I bring encouragement to someone else. That encouragement helps me, and them, to grow in some small way. This growth then teaches me more lessons I need to learn, more ways to love, and guides me back full circle to sharing again.

Share - Encourage - Grow - Learn.

Share - Encourage - Grow - Learn.

Even if you came away from this book with only one morsel of truth that was discovered or reinforced, then share it. That truth will encourage someone else, which will help you both to grow and learn what it is we all need to be doing. Share it. Encourage someone with it. Grow from the experience. Learn what needs to be done next. Then share that.

Even as I speak to you, my children, know in your hearts that your dad loves you. Always has. Always will. The truth gets murky at times, but you will know it in your heart.

Trust your heart.

And share the truth with others.

They need encouragement, too.

Thank you for reading and allowing me to be a part of your growth and learning experience.

Now . . . go share it.

End Notes

i   Marcel Proust (unpublished). *Dynamics of Customer Focus.* Colorado Springs, 2000, p. 1.

Chapter 1
Yoda. Peter McWilliams. *The Portable Do It!* (Los Angeles: Prelude Press, 1995), p. 34.
Emerson. Ibid., p. 131.
David Maraniss. *When Pride Still Mattered.* (New York: Simon & Schuster, 1999), p. 184.

Chapter 2
Auden. Peter McWilliams. *The Portable Do It!* Op cit., p. 196.

Chapter 3
James. Peter McWilliams. *The Portable Do It!* Op cit., p. 159.
Stephen R. Covey. *Principle Centered Leadership.* (New York: Fireside, 1990), p. 67.
Ibid., p. 225.

Chapter 4
William Martin. *The Couples Tao Te Ching.* (New York: Marlowe & Co., 2000), p. 32.
Joel Glenn Brenner. *The Emperor of Chocolate.* (New York: McGraw Hill, 1999), p. 49.
Quoted by Anthony Hopkins in *Instinct.*
Phil Jackson. *Sacred Hoops.* (New York: Hyperion, 1995), p. 69.
Beecher. Peter McWilliams, *The Portable Do It!* Op cit., p. 150.

Chapter 5
Joel Glen Brenner. *The Emperor's of Chocolate.* Op cit., p. 26.
Shaw. Stephen Covey. *Principle Centered Leadership.* Op cit., 324.
Vittorio. Christopher Robbins. *The Test of Courage.* (New York: Free Press, 1999), p. 326.

Chapter 6
Anchee Min. *Becoming Madame Mao.* (New York: Houghton Mifflin, 2000), p. 14.
Richard Foster. *Celebration of Discipline.* (New York: Harper Collins, 1978), p. 33.
Christopher Robbins. *The Test of Courage.* Op cit., p. 332.
Mark Helprin. *Memoir.*
Stephen Lundin as quoted in *American Way,* Oc. 1, 2002, p. 100.

Chapter 7
DeFenelon. Peter McWilliams. *The Portable Do It!* Op cit., p. 56.
Paul Tournier. *Guilt & Grace.* (New York: Harper & Row, 1958), p. 34.

Chapter 8
Jimmy Dean as quoted in *Esquire,* October, 2001.
William Penn as quoted from *QuakerInfo.com.*
Quote from priest in the film *Chocolat.*

Chapter 9

167

Mike Rutherford. *Mike & the Mechanics,* 1988.

Jacob Bronowski. *www.med.yale.edu* as quoted from *The Origin of Knowledge and Imagination* (Yale University Press, 1978).

Gordon MacKenzie. *Orbiting the Giant Hairball.* (New York: Viking Penguin, 1996), p. 53.

Chapter 10

Pedro Calderon de la Barca. *Life is a Dream* (public domain), 1600-1681.

William Martin. *Couples Tao Te Ching.* Op cit., p. 85.

Shakespeare. Joslyn Pine, Ed. *Shakespeare: A Book of Quotations.* (Toronto: Dover, 1998), p. 23.

Chapter 11

Graham. Peter Mac Williams. *The Portable Do It!* Op cit., p. 148.

John J. Ratey, M.D. *A User's Guide to the Brain.* (New York: Pantheon, 2001), p. 364.

Lois. Peter Mac Williams. *The Portable Do It!* Op cit., p. 146.

Chapter 12

Shakespeare. Joslyn Pine, Ed. *Shakespear: A Book of Quotations.* Op cit., 17.

Augustine. St. Augustine. *Day By Day.* (New York: Catholic, 1986), p. 17.

Harris. Peter McWilliams. *The Portable Do It!* Op cit., p. 15.

Chapter 13

Mill. Peter McWilliams. *The Portable Do It!* Op cit., p. 151.

Simon Winchester. *The Map That Changed the World.* (New York: Harper Collins, 2001), p. 25.

Richard Foster. *Celebration of Discipline.* Op cit., p. 1.

Chapter 14

Cowboy Creed. Internet web message (no attribution).

Taylor. Gregg Stebben & Daniel Orange, Ph.D. *Everything You Need to Know About Physics.* (New York: Simon & Schuster, 1999), p. 130.

Chapter 15

Jacob M. Brande. *Complete Speakers & Toastmasters Library.* (New Jersey: Prentice-Hall, 1992), p. 138.

"To Timothy, my true son": I Timothy 1:2.

Quoted from the movie, *On the Water Front.*

"No greater love": John 15:13.

Chapter 16

William Martin. *The Couples Tao Te Ching.* Op cit., p. 58.

Lewis. Richard N. Bolles. *The Three Boxes of Life.* (Berkley: Ten Speed Press, 1978), p. 348.

Cindy Walker & Eddy Arnold. *You Don't Know Me.*

Anchee Min. *Becoming Madame Mao.* Op cit., pp. 7-8.

Josephine Hart. *Damage.* (New York: Ivy Books, 1991), pp. 1-2.

Marlo Morgan. *Mutant Message Down Under.* (New York: Harper Collins, 1991).

Jim Collins. *Good to Great.* (New York: Harper Collins, 2001), p. 62.

Chapter 17

Lyot N. Tolstoi. *My Confession.* (New York: Thomas Y. Crowell Co., 1899), p. 54.

Chapter 19

King. Philip Yancy. *Reaching for the Invisible God.* (Grand Rapids: Zondervan, 2000), p. 233.
Buechner. Ibid., p. 245.
Ibid., p. 229.
Mark Helprin. *Memoir from Antproof Case.* (New York: Wheeler, 1995). P. 514.
David Eggers. *A Heartbreaking Work of Staggering Genius.* (New York: Random House, 2000).
William Martin. *The Couples Tao Te Ching.* Op cit., p. 37.
Nouwen. Philip Yancy. *Reaching for the Invisible God.* Op cit., p. 266.
<u>Chapter 20</u>
Dickson. Peter McWilliams. *The Portable Do It!* Op cit., p. 67.

STEVE WALRATH

Steve Walrath is a 25-year radio broadcast professional. He has worked in all areas of broadcasting including on-air, news, sales, management and owning/managing his own properties. He took over ownership of a 1000-watt AM radio station and, within five years, transformed it into an international corporation of over six divisions, including printing, publishing, broadcasting, catalog center, retail and wholesale travel, computer diagnostics, custom clothing and commercial real estate.

With this success, Steve has taught the principles of Customer Focus, Cultivating Winners from Within, Creating Employee Commitment, Effective Management Skills, and many more topics to such clients as General Motors, Roman Meal Bread Co., Professional Compounding Centers of America, Wisconsin Physicians Service, Trek Bicycles Worldwide, Tombstone Pizza, and hundreds more across the United States, Canada and Australia.

Steve earned both his Bachelors and Masters Degree in Business Management, is a certified instructor in Entrepreneurship for Fast Trac, an instructor for the University of Wisconsin-Small Business Development Center, and is the founder of the D.T.S. Foundation, Inc., holding seminars to help divorced parents protect and preserve their relationship with their kids.

Steve is the author of *"A Divorced Parent's Guide to Seeing Your Kids: what judges, attorneys and your ex have not told you"* and *"Cultivating Winners From Within."* Steve also stays active as Vice President for Crime Stoppers International, is the past president of the YMCA, and numerous other not-for-profit organizations.

His keynotes, workshops and seminars have been rated "A+, relevant to the needs of today. The best speaker this conference has ever had and bring him back for more."

More information can be found at his web site: www.stevewalrath.com

For Seminars, Workshops and Presentations:

D.T.S. Foundation, Inc.
Steve Walrath - Founder
620 Public Ave. • Beloit, WI 53511

Phone: 800.818.DADS
Fax: 608.364.0956
Email: steveradio@charter.net • www.stevewalrath.com

Books, CDs and Support Materials
All purchases are tax-deductible.
Make checks payable to: DTS Foundation, Inc.

1) *Divorced Parent's Guide to Seeing Your Kids: what judges, attorneys and your ex have not told you.* (Soft cover edition) $17.95

2) *Divorced Parent's Guide to Seeing Your Kids– The Seminar as taught by Steve Walrath* (3 CD set with interactive workbook) $49.95

☆ **BONUS:** Divorced Parent Set (#1 & 2) with Steve's best-selling book, plus the seminar CDs & interactive workbook ... *special price of* ... $59.95

3) *Uncommon Sense for Unreasonable Times: How to live a life that matters.* (Soft cover edition) ... $17.95

~ **Special Price when you purchase all 3** ~
$69.00

To order any of the above, call 800.818.DADS or send check or money order to the above address with $3.00 for each item for shipping.

Workshops available from D.T.S. Foundation, Inc.

Keynote Presentations (*or ½-day or 1-day workshops*)
An inspiring set of topics to motivate and challenge your employees, organization, conference, banquet or seminar.

☆ ***Dynamics of Customer Focus*** - This is NOT Customer Service! This is an enlightening, energetic, eye-opening presentation in which all individuals in your organization looks at performing their tasks through the eyes of the customer with a view to adding value to the customer's experience.

☆ ***Cultivating Winners from Within*** - Everyone wants to find the best people to work with. Many times they are sitting right next to us. Learn the secrets to successful People Management which bring diamonds out of the rough and help you recognize and eliminate those who choose not to work within the team system.

☆ ***What Do You Do When Life Just Isn't Fair?*** - Discover and apply the effective principles of how we deal with life's unfair circumstances that create anger, frustration and sometimes despair. Used for adult and student assemblies alike, this unique keynote speech will move the audience to make a difference no matter what life may throw at them.

☆ ***How to Turn Quotes Into Cash*** - Sales is wonderful and challenging, but only if the salesperson masters the skills and attitudes necessary to turn a prospective customer into your paying customer. Learn the inside tips to developing effective sales relationships from a 22-year sales veteran who turned a broadcasting business around from a $10,000 monthly loss to over $500,000 in 3 years!

☆ *The Art of Getting Things Done* - We can only be productive with the skills of managing multiple projects, priorities and deadlines. Learn the principles of time and personal resource management to be the most effective manager and employee possible.

☆ *5+5 = 11 (or more): How to Promote and Market Anything* - The myth of the "used car salesman" is debunked and replaced with the essential elements to make a successful sale and presentation. Learn the principles of why and how we buy including emotion vs. logic and the principle of ownership.

☆ *Supervisory Skills for New Managers* - Employees are only as effective as their managers. This workshop will teach the new supervisor how to successfully coach and lead their staff to greater productivity while creating a team atmosphere. A MUST for all people in their new and challenging position as Manager.

☆ *Using Change as a Catalyst for Growth* - Change is a part of every business–everyday. People, policies, mergers and acquisitions all create change. Your staff and management will learn the principles of successful change that create an atmosphere of trust and move your company forward in a positive and productive manner.

☆ *Overcoming Negativity in Life, Work and Home* - Negativity can creep into anyone's life and work. You will learn the signs of personal, departmental and organizational negativity and how to deal with each effectively. Create a positive environment with positive people!

☆ *Developing a Successful Personal Path in Work, Family and Life* - Life is made up of decisions and changes. How we act, react and interact will determine our path and its satisfaction to us. Learn how to recognize life's little "tests" and how to pass them with flying colors. Take charge of your life rather than letting life happen to you.

☆ **Building a Dynamic New Millennium Organization** - Yes! It can be done, but only if you understand the dynamics of personalities and put into practice effective means of communication. You can take the world's most difficult environment (i.e., a board of directors, your company staff, your organization) and make it dynamic and purposeful.

Dynamics of Customer Focus *(2-day)*
Increase your company's competitive advantage by helping all employees look at the business through eyes of the customer. Employees develop the tools to increase customer focus in their organizations and identify specific customer-focused actions to be implemented.

Customization
Each of our workshops is customized to bring out your individual needs and issues, as well as your specific struggles. The facilitator will discuss your situation in-depth prior to your workshop.